James T. Farrell:
The Revolutionary Socialist Years

Alan M.

THE GOTHAM LIBRARY
OF THE NEW YORK UNIVERSITY PRESS

The Gotham Library is a series of original works and critical studies published in paperback primarily for student use. The Gotham hardcover edition is primarily for use by libraries and the general reader. Devoted to significant works and major authors and to literary topics of enduring importance, Gotham Library texts offer the best in literature and criticism.

Comparative and Foreign Language Literature:
Robert J. Clements, Editor
Comparative and English Language Literature:
James W. Tuttleton, Editor

James T. Farrell about 1944.

James T. Farrell:

The Revolutionary Socialist Years

Alan M. Wald

New York · New York University Press · 1978

Library of Congress Cataloging in Publication Data

Wald, Alan M. 1946-
  James T. Farrell : the revolutionary socialist years.

  (The Gotham library of the New York University Press)
  Bibliography: p.
  Includes index.
  1. Farrell, James Thomas, 1904-   —Political and
social views. 2. Socialism in literature.
PS3511.A738Z93   813'.5'2   77-84156
ISBN 0-8147-9179-4
ISBN 0-8147-9180-8 pbk.

Manufactured in the United States of America

IN MEMORY OF MY TEACHER,
MILTON GOLDBERG (1919-1970)

For Leon Trotsky I felt both admiration and affection. I was not a follower of his in the strict and literal meaning of the term. But I was influenced by him. The Old Man educated some of the members of my generation: I was one of those whom he educated. Were it not for his writings, I would be a different person than I am, and I would think differently than I do.

James T. Farrell, 1940

I began writing my own way, and I shall go on doing it.

This is my first and last word on the subject.

James T. Farrell, 1961

Contents

Acknowledgments

This work would not have been possible without the gracious assistance and support of a large number of individuals. First and foremost among them are George Novack, who planted the idea for this project in a conversation with me in the spring of 1968 when I was a student at Antioch College, and James T. Farrell, who opened up his rich archives and vast memory in the interest of helping me reconstruct, as accurately as possible, the literary and political activities described in this book. They, along with Felix Morrow and Meyer Schapiro, two other important participants in a number of the events discussed, devoted many hours to reading my manuscripts, answering questions, and providing guidance. However, I alone am responsible for the interpretations and any errors or weaknesses in this study.

A number of scholars from various institutions have assisted me at various stages in the writing of this book. They include Henry Nash Smith, Frederick Crews, Edgar Branch, Laurence Goldstein, Patrick Quinn, James Cockcroft, Larzer Ziff, Michael Folsom, James Gilbert, Samuel Haber, and Richard Hutson. Anyone working in the field of American literary radicalism must pay tribute to the importance of Daniel Aaron's pioneering work *Writers on the Left: Episodes in American Literary Communism* (1961). Despite the fact that part of my motivation for undertaking this study was to augment Aaron's book and offer a new perspective on the role of Farrell and other anti-Stalinist radical intellectuals, my debt to Aaron is significant. It was his book which suggested to me the method of first-hand encounters with a spectrum of people involved in political-literary controversies, and which provided models for analyzing and integrating private correspondence, public political statements, and imaginative literature.

The indisputable high point of my research was a series of personal interviews granted to me by Hal Draper, F. W. Dupee, James T. Farrell, Albert Glotzer, Sara Jacobs, Dwight Macdonald, John McDonald, Felix Morrow, George Novack, William Phillips, Meyer Schapiro, Adelaide Walker, and Bernard Wolfe. Some of these meetings were made possible by financial assistance from the University of California at Berkeley and the University of Michigan. Special funding from Berkeley also permitted me to do research in the Farrell Collection at the University of Pennsylvania. There I was competently assisted by Dr. Neda Westlake and her staff in examining materials from which Mr. Farrell has given me permission to quote. A grant from the American Council of Learned Societies enabled me to study the papers of Herbert Solow in Ajijic, Jalisco, Mexico.

I am also indebted to my wife, Celia, and to a number of personal friends who gave me aid: George Breitman, Peter Graumann, Ralph Levitt, Jack Alan Robbins, Michael Tormey, and Jac Wasserman. In addition to the people I interviewed, those individuals who were kind enough to provide me with information by mail include Lionel Abel, Sherry Abel, James Atlas, Louis Berg, Earle Birney, James Burnham, Eleanor Clark, Malcolm Cowley, Lewis Feuer, Clement Greenberg, Louis Hacker, Albert Halper, Elinor Rice Hays, Granville Hicks, Sidney Hook, Irving Howe, Quincy Howe, Harold Isaacs, Paul Jacobs, Matthew Josephson, Suzanne La Follette, Mary McCarthy, Arthur Mizener, Miriam Patchen, Victor Perlo, Stanley Plastrik, Philip Rahv, Winifred Rorty, Harold Rosenberg, Harry Roskolenko, Muriel Rukeyser,

Jack Salzman, Paul Siegel, Bette Swados, Diana Trilling, Lionel Trilling, Jean van Heijenoort, Stan Weir, and George Weissman.

Some portions of this book appeared in a different form in the essay "Farrell and Trotskyism" in *Twentieth Century Literature*, 22 (February 1976), 90-104.

Chronology

1904
On February 27, James Thomas Farrell is born in Chicago. His father, a teamster, is too poor to provide adequately for the entire family and, in 1907, Farrell is taken to live with his grandparents in a middle-class environment.

1925
In June, Farrell begins studies at the University of Chicago, at which he is periodically enrolled until the summer of 1929. In this period, after studying with Professor James Weber Linn, Farrell decides to become a writer.

1927
On August 22, the anarchists Sacco and Vanzetti are executed in Boston.

1928
In January, Leon Trotsky is exiled to Alma Ata in Turkestan; a year later he is forced to leave the Soviet Union.

1932

In April, Farrell and his first wife (Dorothy Butler) arrive in New York City after a year in Paris. The first volume of the Studs Lonigan trilogy is published that same month.

1935

In April, Farrell's association with the Communist party is at its high point when he addresses the first American Writers' Congress in New York City.

1936

In May, *A Note on Literary Criticism* is published and Farrell's debate with Communist writers is intensified. Between July 17 and 21, the fascist uprising begins in Morocco and spreads to Spain. That fall, the first volume of the O'Neill-O'Flaherty series is published.

1937

In April, Farrell, a member of the Executive Committee of the American Committee for the Defense of Leon Trotsky, goes to Mexico to observe the hearings of the John Dewey Commission of Inquiry. In December, *Partisan Review,* formerly a John Reed Club organ, is re-launched on an independent basis.

1939

On August 24, the Hitler-Stalin Pact is signed. In the fall a dispute breaks out in the Socialist Workers party between the followers of Cannon and the followers of Shachtman. This culminates in a split and Shachtman forms the Workers party as a rival group in April 1940. Although more sympathetic to Cannon's party at first, Farrell maintains relations with both organizations.

1940

On August 21, Leon Trotsky is assassinated by an agent of Stalin's GPU.

1941

In January, Farrell marries the actress Hortense Alden. Later that year he becomes chairman of the Civil Rights Defense Committee, which defends members of the Socialist Workers party and of Minneapolis Teamsters Local 544 who have been indicted under the Smith Act.

1946
In May, the first of the Bernard Carr novels is published.

1948
In April, Farrell issues a statement supporting the Marshall Plan. Having broken with the Socialist Workers party several years earlier, Farrell now separates from the Workers party as well.

List of Illustrations

5. Suzanne La Follette, Benjamin Stolberg, Otto Ruhle and John Dewey during the Dewey Commission hearings in Coyoacan, Mexico, in April 1937. Courtesy of James T. Farrell.

6. Jan Frankel, James T. Farrell, Albert Glotzer, Bernard Wolfe and Dorothy Eisner at the home of Frida Kahlo and Diego Rivera in Mexico in April 1937. Courtesy of Albert Glotzer.

7. James P. Cannon, Martin Abern and Max Shachtman outside the Socialist Workers party offices at 116 University Place in New York City in 1938.

8. James T. Farrell speaking at the Farewell Banquet for the Minneapolis Eighteen on December 26, 1943. At left: Farrell Dobbs. At right: Alfred Russell, Ted Grant and Karl Kuehn. Courtesy of Pathfinder Press.

9. James P. Cannon, Felix Morrow and Albert Goldman in the Minneapolis headquarters of the Socialist Workers party before surrendering to U.S. marshals on December 31, 1943. Courtesy of Pathfinder Press.

10. George Novack, secretary of the Civil Rights Defense Committee, in Washington D.C. on April 2, 1944, to present petitions and resolutions to Presidential Pardon Authority, demanding pardon of the Minneapolis labor case prisoners. Courtesy of Pathfinder Press.

11. James T. Farrell and Hortense Alden in the 1940s. Courtesy of James T. Farrell.

12. James T. Farrell addressing Welcome Home meeting for the Minneapolis labor case prisoners at the Hotel Diplomat in New York City on February 2, 1945. Left to right: Oscar Schoenfeld, Karl Kuehn, George Novack, Farrell Dobbs (behind speaker), James T. Farrell (at podium), Felix Morrow, Albert Goldman. Courtesy of Pathfinder Press.

Introduction: The Complementary Side of Farrell

James T. Farrell's "Note on Literary Criticism" is quite a remarkable event. ... one is surprised, after reading Mr. Farrell's novels, which derive so much of their effectiveness from the total immersion of the author in the lives of unreflecting and limited people, to discover behind them a mind capable of philosophical abstractions and analysis.

Edmund Wilson, 1936[1]

Four decades of scholarship and criticism have established the literary stature of James T. Farrell's three cycles of novels centering around Studs Lonigan, the O'Neill and O'Flaherty families, and Bernard Carr.[2] Dissertations and essays have traced the doctrinal root of this achievement to Farrell's naturalism, which he formulated in the late 1920s from his studies of John Dewey, George Herbert Mead, C. Judson Herrick, and William James. Previous studies have also noted the impact on Farrell of the ideas of

1

Thorstein Veblen, R.H. Tawney, Friedrich Nietzsche, Sigmund
Freud, Walter Pater, and Bertrand Russell. Finally, critics and
scholars have demonstrated the thematic, technical, and inspira-
tional influences of Sherwood Anderson, Theodore Dreiser, H.L.
Mencken, Sinclair Lewis, Anton Chekhov, Marcel Proust, James
Joyce, Ernest Hemingway, and John Dos Passos.[3]

The more sophisticated studies—especially the scholarship of
Edgar Branch—have highlighted Farrell's intellectual formation in
the late 1920s: his renunciation of religion, his reading of realists
and modernists, his philosophical and historical interests leading to
his assimilation of pragmatism and naturalism. They have also
indicated Farrell's prominent role during the 1930s and 1940s as a
Marxist-oriented opponent of Stalinism. But at the same time as
such a significant body of scholarship has been devoted to this
urban realist as a literary interpreter of the naturalism and
pragmatism of Dewey, Mead, and James in the Studs Lonigan,
O'Neill-O'Flaherty, and Bernard Carr cycles, some of the most
stirring and distinguished contributions of James T. Farrell to
American intellectual history and Marxist literary theory have
remained sorely underdeveloped. The fact that Leon Trotsky's
revolutionary internationalist ideas appealed so strongly to a
native American realist during his most productive years is in itself
a phenomenon that deserves attention.

This book is a literary, political, and intellectual portrait of
James T. Farrell during his revolutionary socialist years. It traces
his evolution from the late 1920s until the late 1940s, when there
began a new and different stage in his development. Receiving
special attention in the book are Farrell's intellectual roots in the
late 1920s; his literary conflicts with the Communist movement
between 1932 and 1936; his role in the American Committee for
the Defense of Leon Trotsky; various aspects of his relations with
Partisan Review magazine; and his activities in opposition to United
States government policy during the Second World War. A
discussion of George Novack's friendship and correspondence with
Farrell is used to elucidate Farrell's ties to Trotskyism during the
1930s, and a parallel examination involving Meyer Schapiro is
used to clarify Farrell's attitudes toward the intellectual left during
the 1940s.

The study's closing sections demonstrate the importance of the involvement with Trotskyism for Farrell's intellectual development, his literary criticism, and certain secondary aspects of his achievement in fiction. The conclusion emphasizes how Farrell's decisive intellectual formation in the 1920s—his immersion in the ideas of the liberal pragmatists (especially those of John Dewey)—helped to propel him toward Trotskyism, yet ultimately, in conjunction with world-historic events, prevented total acceptance of Trotsky's doctrine.

An additional dimension of this book is that it attempts to put Farrell's evolution into perspective as paradigmatic of a group of prominent New York intellectuals. Here I must point out that this book is a central component of a broader study which I have been conducting for a number of years. The larger project is a chronicle and assessment of American writers who were influenced in various ways by Leon Trotsky during the 1930s and 1940s. These figures constituted a heterogeneous yet distinct group which, with certain qualifications, can be called the "Trotskyist intellectuals." Included were a number of talented literary critics, journalists, poets, philosophers, historians, and novelists.

Many from this group rose to prominence in their fields, giving the Trotskyist experience (however limited and transient it may have been in some individual cases) a discernible impact on American culture. The prestige of figures such as Sidney Hook, Meyer Schapiro, Louis Hacker, and Saul Bellow is indisputable. The founders of *Partisan Review, Commentary,* and *Dissent* magazines were veterans of this Trotskyist experience. Furthermore, Charles Kadushin's recent study, *The American Intellectual Elite* (1974), contains the results of a poll of American intellectuals who elected the following eleven as their outstanding peers: Mary McCarthy, Irving Howe, Dwight MacDonald, Lionel Trilling, Edmund Wilson, Norman Mailer, Susan Sontag, Daniel Bell, Noam Chomsky, John Kenneth Galbraith, and Robert Silvers. The first six on the list were touched by Trotskyism, and two of them held membership for a while in Trotskyist parties.

Of course, those who accepted the full program of Trotsky's ideas, committing themselves to party work for a substantial number of years or for their entire lives, were few. And these individuals had little opportunity for accomplishment in broader intellectual arenas. Men such as George Novack, Sherry Mangan, Felix Morrow, Albert Goldman, and Joseph Vanzler made their main intellectual contributions inside the Trotskyist movement. They cannot be assessed in the same manner as those for whom association with Trotskyism was just a passing influence on their development.

However, it would be a mistake to assume that those who held party membership only briefly, or who were just peripherally involved, bore insignificant marks of the experience in later years. In three previously published essays cited in the bibliography ("Revolutionary Intellectuals: *Partisan Review* in the 1930s," "The *Menorah* Group Moves Left," and "Herbert Solow: Portrait of a New York Intellectual"), I have demonstrated that these individuals comprised a group with a pattern of some identifiable characteristics in its origins, political involvement, and subsequent intellectual activities. Some of these characteristics are reviewed in the introduction and conclusion of this book for, despite his unique attributes, James T. Farrell embodied many representative qualities of the Trotskyist intellectuals and became one of their central organizers and spokesmen. But, in addition to his political role in the group, Farrell is a novelist of significant stature in his own right and has been prolific in the production of critical and polemical essays. Therefore, an examination of his writing has intrinsic value as literary history and also constitutes a primary source for the study of Trotsky's impact and the problems confronted by the group of Trotskyist intellectuals.

Two potential difficulties may be encountered by the reader of this book. The first stems from its close integration of literary and political matters. The second is rooted in the need to understand the broader group of Trotskyist intellectuals and Farrell's role vis-à-vis that group. In the first case, although every attempt has been made to eliminate unnecessary political jargon and allusions, politics and political events were central for the individuals and period under consideration. It is mandatory that every student of radical intellectuals in the 1930s should, at the least, be familiar with the terms connected with the major political turns of the Communist International.

Although there is not space for elaboration, the following should be kept in mind: Between 1924 and 1928 the Communist International underwent a process of transformation, during which a faction of the Bolshevik party represented by the political outlook and person of Joseph Stalin became dominant. The term "Stalinism" refers to the official Communist movement during and after that time. The "Third Period" was the term used by Communists throughout the world to describe the six years after 1928, which were thought to be the final ones for capitalism. Communist tactics internationally during the Third Period were marked by ultraleftism and extreme sectarianism. In particular, the Communists dubbed the Socialist movement "Social Fascist," they constructed dual unions, and they advocated the "United Front from Below" (which meant willingness to collaborate only with the ranks but not the leaders of non-Communist organizations). In 1935, however, the international Communist movement, reeling from the disaster in Germany at the hands of Hitler, turned dramatically to the right. It announced the Popular Front policy of building coalition governments of workers parties and liberal capitalist parties. In the view of Trotskyist and left-wing Socialist critics, this new strategy meant subordinating the independent struggles of workers in capitalist countries to the diplomatic needs of the Soviet rulers.

The second problem—that of explaining Farrell's precise relation to the group of Trotskyist intellectuals—might be partially overcome by considering the following background material. Leon Trotsky achieved his first significant following among American radical literary intellectuals during the 1920s. By the end of the decade, however, former admirers such as Michael Gold and Joseph Freeman had suppressed their respect for Trotsky in public writings out of subservience to the Communist party line. But Max Eastman achieved international prominence, as well as ostracism by the American Left, for his defense of Trotskyism and his translations of Trotsky's works. Also during the late 1920s and early 1930s, there emerged a group of independent Marxist intellectuals who collaborated with the Communist party in New York City. At first they thought they could influence the Communist party by supporting it, but they came into increasing conflicts with Stalinist Third Period policy (especially as it was being applied in Germany). Most notable among this largely academic group was Sidney Hook, who had prodigious intellectual prestige in leftwing circles. His influence extended into a coterie of young Jewish writers whom Elliot Cohen had gathered around the *Menorah Journal.*

The break of these New York intellectuals from the Communist party was announced publicly in February 1934 in an open letter castigating the party's disruption of a Socialist mass meeting. From the former *Menorah Journal* group, Herbert Solow and Felix Morrow (along with two friends, George Novack and John McDonald) joined the Trotskyists; Elliot Cohen, Anita Brenner, and Louis Berg collaborated with the Trotskyists in the Non-Partisan Labor Defense Committee until it was dissolved in 1936. Sidney Hook worked closely with the Trotskyists on several occasions, but he was more accurately part of a current including Lewis Corey (the pen name of Louis Fraina, one of the founders of American Communism), Louis Hacker, James Rorty, V.F. Calverton, and Meyer Schapiro, whose main object became that of constructing an active left-wing opposition to the Stalinists. These were the elements of the already existing movement of anti-Stalinist radical intellectuals which James T. Farrell would openly join in 1936. A year later he was followed by the editors of the reorganized *Partisan Review.*

The following history might also be of aid to distinguish some of the characteristics of the intellectuals influenced by Trotskyism from those of writers who identified with the Communist movement. The Communist party began the 1930s with a "proletarian culture" orientation that was led and directed by Michael Gold, Joseph Freeman, and Joshua Kunitz.[4] These men had sustained left-wing literary activity during the 1920s and their influence was dependent on their positions in the increasingly bureaucratized United States arm of the Third International. As the Depression deepened, the Communist party soon attracted a sizable following of young and unknown writers, many of plebeian backgrounds. For such neophytes, the Stalinist organization often sufficed as an elementary school of literature and politics, and the students learned instinctively that submission to rules and requirements was rewarded by a place in print, comradeship, and a ready-made audience.[5]

The Communists also gained the allegiance of two other groups in the early thirties. First, there was a smattering of quondam literary exiles and aesthetes such as Malcolm Cowley and Matthew Josephson. After renouncing the "religion of art," which had "died in theory with the Dada movement and in practice with the world crisis of capitalism," they gravitated toward what they thought was the Red Parnassus of a new epoch of literary development.[6] Then there were writers such as Theodore Dreiser, Sherwood Anderson, Sinclair Lewis, John Dos Passos, and Edmund Wilson. Being more established figures and, in some cases, a bit older, the members of this group were independently positioned so that they could maintain looser, less restricted, and sometimes idiosyncratic connections with the Stalinists. (The last two traveled steadily toward an antagonistic stance which became explicit by the time of the Moscow Trials; Theodore Dreiser did join the party, but it was only briefly, at the close of his life.)

In contrast, the intellectual origins of the outstanding Trotskyist and left-wing anti-Stalinist writers of the 1930s began with the independent assimilation of certain social and cultural notions in the 1920s. These often were derived from an understanding of contemporary materialist philosophy and social theory and respect for the functions of imaginative literature beyond immediately apparent usages and meanings. As an incipient group, these energetic intellectuals had often achieved unusual breadth, depth and self-sufficiency prior to the Depression, and hence they were better prepared to assess Communist party policy from a critical stance. For most, the route to radical anti-Stalinism in the 1930s included ill-fated attempts at collaboration with the Stalinized Communist party in sympathizer organizations such as the League of Professionals (originally a support group for the 1932 Communist presidential and vice-presidential candidates) and the National Committee for the Defense of Political Prisoners.

In the 1920s, those attending Columbia undergraduate and/or graduate school included Herbert Solow, Meyer Schapiro, Lionel Trilling, Sidney Hook, Louis Hacker, Harold Isaacs, Felix Morrow, and, earlier, Max Eastman (around 1910). Passing through

Harvard in the same decade were John Wheelwright, Sherry Mangan, George Novack, Joseph Vanzler, and, earlier, Benjamin Stolberg and John Dos Passos. F.W. Dupee, John Chamberlain, Dwight Macdonald, Elliot Cohen, and Bernard Wolfe attended Yale, while Edmund Wilson and James Burnham studied at Princeton. Among the women who achieved some prominence in this circle, Mary McCarthy, Eleanor Clark, and Nancy Mac-Donald attended Vassar. Of course there were some exceptions to this patrician educational background—James T. Farrell, Philip Rahv, and William Phillips being the most important.

A good number of these intellectuals concentrated their studies in the humanities, and a significant common denominator for many of them was a close acquaintance with the ideas of John Dewey and often with the man himself. Max Eastman and Sidney Hook worked under Dewey while completing their doctoral studies at Columbia; Meyer Schapiro was also a student of Dewey and aided him on chapters of *Art as Experience* (1934); Herbert Solow was close to Dewey; James T. Farrell studied Dewey at the University of Chicago with Edwin A. Burtt in 1926 and three years later commenced a thorough reading program of Dewey's major works.[7] By 1937, there coalesced a self-reliant group which had no lack of authentic scholars (such as Sidney Hook, Meyer Schapiro, and Louis Hacker), and which was animated by an articulate corps of oral and journalistic polemicists (such as Philip Rahv, Herbert Solow, James T. Farrell, Max Eastman, Elliot Cohen, and Benjamin Stolberg).

More than most other radical writers who made their debut in the Depression decade, James Thomas Farrell (who was born in 1904) was intellectually prepared for the 1930s. He provided himself with a strong background in social as well as literary theory. Since this achievement represented exertion of enormous willpower—he had to fight against his religious upbringing and the commoner's destiny in Chicago's South Side—its expressions were sometimes clumsy; yet its durability was remarkable.

Farrell was atypical of the group that became Trotskyist intellectuals for three reasons: because of his Irish plebeian origins, his personal struggle against Catholicism, and his unique rise to fame in the early 1930s as an outstanding exponent of the urban realistic novel. In many cases, the other members of the group came from immigrant Jewish backgrounds. Few of them achieved notice outside of academic or professional circles until the 1940s. Most of those in and around the group who eventually wrote fiction—Saul Bellow, Mary McCarthy, Bernard Wolfe, Lionel Trilling, Eleanor Clark, Edmund Wilson, Isaac Rosenfeld—did not choose the common people as their subject nor realism-naturalism as their method.

Nevertheless, Farrell shared the most crucial features with the group. During the 1920s he assimilated the philosophical pragmatism of John Dewey, as well as experimental technical innovations of Joyce, Hemingway, and other literary modernists. (But in the latter case it must be noted that Farrell remained thoroughly committed to the school of Anderson, Dreiser, and Lewis in literary goals and subject matter. The literary basis of Farrell's eventual drift away from *Partisan Review* was not a blanket rejection of modernism of his part, but his firm belief that realism-naturalism still remained the most central and progressive tradition.)

Furthermore, in the political struggles of the 1930s, Farrell shared with other figures in the group an attachment to Leon Trotsky as a Promethean champion of truth, as a sophisticated ally in combat against both Stalinist and commercial literary pressures, and as an authoritative critic of Communist policy (especially in Germany, where the Communist line tended to disorient resistance to Hitler, and in Spain and France, where the interests of the workers were subordinated to Soviet foreign policy). Other aspects of Trotskyism which the group found attractive included Trotsky's contributions to Marxist political theory and literary criticism. In the realm of political theory they were especially impressed with the theory of Permanent Revolution, which explained the possibility of bourgeois revolutions being transformed into socialist revolutions in underdeveloped countries. In the area of aesthetics they appreciated Trotsky's openness to literary experimentation—and his opposition to judging art by political criteria—as expressed in *Literature and Revolution* (1924). In his relation to Trotsky, Farrell was differentiated from the bulk of the anti-Stalinist radical intellectuals primarily by his collaborating with the American Trotskyists more openly and consistently, and in his remaining by his Marxist convictions several years longer than his contemporaries.

This book does not attempt to recapitulate or give synopses of the substantial body of literary criticism that has appeared in scores of studies about Farrell as the author of the Studs Lonigan trilogy and other important works in American fiction. Rather, the focus is on the complementary "other side" of Farrell, which includes a noteworthy body of fictional, dramatic, poetic, theoretical, critical, historical, polemical, biographical, and autobiographical writing about the role and responsibility of the socially committed writer and literary intellectual. Farrell wrote the bulk (but not the entirety) of this material between the time he returned from Paris in the spring of 1932, and his reassessment of the revolutionary socialist project around 1948. The importance of this phase in Farrell's still continuing career as a writer and critic, and of its role in shaping the American intellectual left, is a matter of record, even if it has never been intensively examined before. As George Novack, a former political associate of Farrell, reminisced:

> It's right to give a distinct and central place and role to Farrell [in a study of intellectuals influenced by Trotsky] because he was one of the most prominent, productive, and energetic of all the writers. . . . Farrell had a stronger character than most of his contemporaries, a greater independence and critical mindedness. He showed the same dogged determination and single-mindedness in promoting his political ideas and his views on literary criticism as he did in sticking to his subject and style of writing. He was not easily swerved from his course once he was convinced of its correctness.[8]

Due to the high premium placed on detail, I have chosen to work within the confines of certain limitations. Most significantly, the consequences of Farrell's dramatic political change in the late 1940s and after are not probed. I made this decision partly because the problems and responses of intellectuals during the Cold War era are indicative of such a different historical dilemma that I have reserved the subject for a separate and different kind of study. Furthermore, even though this book focuses on Farrell as a revolutionary intellectual and crusader aspiring to transform a world he never made, it does not consider his heroic battles against literary censorship and it treats only peripherally much of Farrell's fiction about the problems of writers and intellectuals which are not especially political (or which seem to be derived from his Parisian or European experiences). Furthermore, Farrell was a man with an extraordinarily wide range of personal friends and intellectual and political acquaintances. The fact that this study considers almost exclusively his association with radicals should not obscure or negate the importance of Farrell's other relationships—for example, those with nonsocialist or conservative figures (such as William Troy or H.L. Mencken,) and those with family members, childhood friends, and acquaintances from the 1920s.

In conclusion, a study of what I have described as the "complementary side of James T. Farrell" is intended to be just that: It is designed to complement the already existing treatments of Farrell's philosophical naturalism and major early novels. These earlier examinations of Farrell's literary and intellectual ideas and writings confirm his ineradicable place in American letters. The purpose of this book is to revivify his dynamic role in the literary left, in the American experience with Marxist thought, and in the struggle of writers and intellectuals to forge an effective role for themselves in the movement for revolutionary social change—a struggle which was largely frustrated by powerful national and world forces beyond their control.

1.

Emergence from the Twenties

In a commercial civilization, where the dollar is stressed and where universal acquisitiveness breeds universal suspicion, there is little question as to which problems are most important. . . . there must be a form of social organization that directs what is most generous and social in man and that sublimates what is not. In brief, the problem of those of us who own the thirties is more one of social attack than of ethical reversion and traditionalism.

James T. Farrell, 1930 [1]

In late October 1958, James T. Farrell surveyed the beginning of a prose manuscript and judged the time appropriate to start a new phase in his career as an artist—a new struggle to produce the kind of fiction he valued. He reaffirmed this resolve and began a new series of books, despite nearly a decade of having been neglected by a commercially oriented publishing industry. Seven years later, Farrell codified some of his thoughts on this decision when he composed an introduction to *When Time Was Born,* a prose-poem component of his vast new project, "A Universe of Time." There Farrell reasserted his lifelong conviction that "Neither God nor man is going to tell me what to write":[2]

> They can fight me as they wish. They can blacklist me as they wish. They can reject me as they wish.
>
> I guarantee to survive, and, I guarantee that my bones, dissolving into chalky dust, will fight them from the grave.[3]

The result of this reconfirmation has included the publication of several semi-autobiographical works requisite for understanding his intellectual formation during his early twenties, the period of growth in which the precepts coalesced which would guide him during the Great Depression. In the late 1920s, Farrell lived primarily in Chicago. After six quarters of outstanding academic work at the University of Chicago, mainly in the social sciences, Farrell hitchhiked to New York City to write and work for six months. When he returned, he studied composition at the university and was employed as a reporter for the *Chicago Herald Examiner*. He traveled briefly again to New York in the early fall of 1929, and then in April 1931 eloped to Paris with Dorothy Butler, where they spent exactly one year. During that time *Young Lonigan*, which had been rejected by Clifton Fadiman for Simon and Schuster, was accepted by James Henle of Vanguard Press, to which it had been submitted by Walt Carmon (Farrell's friend, who was then the managing editor of the Communist *New Masses*).[4]

Most important in the body of imaginative literature that records the unfolding of Farrell's intellect are two novels, *The Silence of History* (1963) and *Lonely for the Future* (1966), and *The Collected Poems of James T. Farrell* (1965). Of secondary importance are *A Brand New Life* (1968), and two novels written earlier but published in the 1960s: *Boarding House Blues* (1961) and *New Year's Eve/1929* (1967). In conjunction with two major novels completed in the 1940s—*My Days of Anger* (1943) and *Bernard Clare* (1946)—this total of eight works almost completes the representation of the vital social and intellectual forces which shaped the consciousness of the young Farrell. (Here it must be remarked that the unifying characters of most of these novels, Danny O'Neill and Eddie Ryan, are to a large degree fictional autobiographical representations of Farrell himself. Bernard Carr is a different case, although some of Carr's experiences and feelings resemble those of Farrell. In discussing the books featuring these characters I have decided that, when there seems to be sufficient evidence, it is justifiable to treat certain episodes as if they were almost straight autobiography.)

Farrell's development, as represented by Ryan and O'Neill, is portrayed in several sequences from *The Silence of History* to *Boarding House Blues.* Nourished by readings that included Sinclair Lewis' *Babbitt,* Walter Pater's "Conclusion" to *The Renaissance,* and studies of Napoleon and the French Revolution, the autobiographical character experiences a profound intellectual awakening during 1925 and 1926 in *The Silence of History.* Four years later, in *Boarding House Blues,* his philosophic outlook has matured to a conscious rejection of a hedonistic interpretation of Nietzsche and a repudiation of romantic and mechanical faith in "religious" socialism (each of which had been a viewpoint advocated by two friends). O'Neill's new outlook is animated by a respect for science, knowledge, and the dignity of the oppressed of humanity. In 1973 Farrell recollected that

> It would be nonsense to think that it was my experience in New York that made me a radical. I was thinking about those kinds of questions long before. 'n 1926, in Chicago, I gave a speech on Marx. I expected the Depression and predicted a new war. Also, in 1926, at the University of Chicago, I spoke denouncing racism, supporting civil rights, and advocating municipalization of housing to halt discrimination.[5]

Farrell wrote *The Silence of History* as the foundation for his new series, but the novel stands alone as a psychologically penetrating study of the factors in his intellectual composition during the 1920s.[6] He combines technical innovations in language and form, inspired by Joyce, Proust, Dos Passos, Hemingway, and others, with characteristic philosophical themes. He centers the novel around the multiple significance of one act on a July day in 1926, when Eddie Ryan resigns from his job as an attendant in a

Chicago service station. Eddie's act seems an almost unnatural mystery to him, because it involves a conscious rejection of possible success which he craves. (Eddie is favored by his superiors, and promotions and financial rewards seem likely.) Furthermore, the immediate consequences of the decision entail his taking risks that could result in multiple complications for his personal life.

All the factors involved in this choice are scrutinized, and Eddie's intellectual development during the previous year is recaptured to communicate not just the nature of his one act, but the nature of human actions in general. Farrell's appreciation of the half-willed, half-determined aspects of such acts and their ultimate significance is indicated explicitly in "The Notebook of Danny O'Neill," which comprises Part III of *Boarding House Blues:*

> Destinies are made up of the happenings of a life. These follow one after the other, the phrase to use is "in serial order". . . . This "serial order" of happenings, in a person's life, lead up to his destiny. They do not add up, but accumulate, not in any pile, but in a tendency, a direction, and they are like the "cometogether"—currents that compose the current of the wind. A life is blown by a wind called destiny, and that wind is controlled by the mind as much as by circumstances.[7]

A critical assessment of *The Silence of History* must acknowledge that several lengthy passages make dull reading and seem to possess only an oblique connection to the central concern of the novel. Nevertheless, there is an essential unity of theme and form in *The Silence of History.* The book poses a philosophical problem (the relationship of the individual to history) which it gradually centers and roots in complex social reality. The experience of reading the novel itself conveys precisely this complexity of the "cometogether" of destiny.

Eddie grows impressively through his reading during 1925. He becomes increasingly conscious of the world around him, the forces that shape it, and particularly the "Tyranny of Time" which steals the future from him even as he watches the seconds tick by. Gradually he is seized by a desire to enrich these seconds. Eddie's temperament has been saddened by the memory of his father: " . . .

his stricken, broken father, dragging death itself along." [8] Now he perceives that it is through the intense awareness of the social and biological tragedy of life that the transcendence of the artist becomes possible, and he aspires to write in order to reach for the vision of the "Conclusion" of Pater's *The Renaissance:*

> No moment should pass in boredom. No minute should escape from a human being's life wasted and unused. Each moment should have value and equality: to be dull and bored was to squander God's greatest gift.[9]

Although he has come from a culturally barren background, Eddie discovers that he can learn if he applies himself with sufficient concentration at night school (as Farrell did briefly, at De Paul University).[10] Gradually he becomes ambitious for the kind of middle-class "success" associated with money and social prestige. But in the course of *The Silence of History*, these ambitions become transformed into a desire for a "success" defined by intellectual and cultural fulfillment. Crucial in the transitional process is Eddie's awareness, nurtured by readings of Sinclair Lewis and other realists, of the need to shed illusions. These experiences prepare Eddie for the deep-felt personal understanding he achieved when studying Napoleon and the French Revolution:

> The French Revolution, as it was described and analyzed in class and in Eddie's readings, cleared his mind of platitudes, fragmented impressions, like torn bits of old letters or notebooks, remembered clichés and lurid, melodramatic scenes of savage murder and brutality.[11]

Eddie's examination of the life of Napoleon leaves him awed by the dynamism and accomplishments of the man, but he is also touched by the philosophic meanings embedded in Napoleon's ultimate defeat and exile: "On St. Helena, Napoleon must håve heard the wind, and heard the ocean waves rushing and breaking on rocky shores, and he must have heard the silence of history." [12] Thus Eddie, suffering an ordeal of endless study, absorbing thought, and piercing self-scrutiny, comes to a stage where he is able to strip himself of the most deep-seated illusion, an unmasking that is prerequisite to his spiritual liberation: He perceives that one's life and accomplishments, no matter how glorious, are eternally restricted to the realm of the real living world. Ultimately humanity must confront an impassive universe of corrosive time and a relentless historical process. It is only through assimilating this reality that one can attain the perspective and passion to experience the enriched life of the artist in which one literally feels the quality of the passing moments.

Following the terms of grinding study (often augmented by a fifty-four-hour work week) recorded in *The Silence of History,* Eddie Ryan enters a new phase described in *Lonely for the Future.* Supported and partially incited by his friend George Raymond, Eddie frequents a working-class Bohemian social club on the South Side of Chicago; he also subscribes to a rowdyish application of certain of Nietzsche's ideas (contained, for example, in *Thus Spoke Zarathustra*) which George Raymond interprets as arguments for amoral behavior.[13] But the function of the novel is to delineate the means by which Eddie becomes increasingly aware that, although he admires the ebullient daring of George's "Nietzscheanism," he is equally repelled by the way George can construe Nietzsche to justify his abuse of people. Eddie's motivation for his rambunctious life with George has been the desire for educational experience and adventure; the next step (in the book as in real life) will be the hitchhike to New York City. Eddie tries to assume an amoral stance as he watches George deceive a homosexual, seduce a misled virgin and antagonize her dull-witted but loyal boyfriend. But in line with the general mood of intellectuals in the late 1920s, who were tiring of the frivolousness and waste of the decade, Eddie becomes increasingly disconcerted. The book is not conclusive, although Eddie is shown as clearly on the road first to a rejection of George's interpretation of Nietzsche, and then to a rebellion directed at very specific social ills.

Farrell took a corresponding attitude of critical assimilation toward the socialism he encountered. This was the pre-World War I Debsian Social Democratic variety, which he perceived as both religious and as economic determinism. It is in *Boarding House Blues* that Farrell (Danny O'Neill) dramatizes his opposition to both

philosophic outlooks: one inspired by the hedonistic Nietzscheanism of George Raymond (in this book called Ed Lanson) and the
other by the romantic, economic determinist socialism of Bill
Bailey.[14] An indication of this coming confrontation appeared in
Lonely for the Future, when Eddie declared: "John, socialism might
be inevitable, but it won't save mankind. Mankind can't be
saved." The implication seems to be that Eddie was intellectually
prepared to accept the conception of socialism as a historic stage of
social evolution—in the way that capitalism succeeded feudalism,
as a more advanced system—but only from a scientific perspective,
and not from a religious faith in socialism perceived as a millennial
salvation.

In many places in the O'Neill-O'Flaherty series, names of
Marxist leaders and references to socialism are sprinkled in as
background. However, in My Days of Anger (a novel which was also
about Farrell's University of Chicago period in the mid-1920s),
questions about socialism, Marxism, the Russian Revolution are
offered as incipient intellectual concerns of Danny. In particular,
there is a classroom debate scene where Danny first grasps
Marxism as an intellectual tool, a method, although his skeptical
mind instinctively produces a hostile response.[15]

In 1927, Farrell was in New York and came upon an issue of the
New Masses featuring a story on the imprisoned anarchists Sacco
and Vanzetti. Farrell participated in the famous Union Square
demonstration protesting their execution. His emotions at the time
were probably similar to those described in a moving thirteen-page
section of Bernard Clare.[16] The impact on the novel's protagonist
(who in this instance resembles Farrell) is largely emotional, and it
is only in Boarding House Blues, covering a period approximately
three years later, that a maturation in the autobiographical figure
seems to be evident. Both Bill Bailey and Ed Lanson, as well as the
whole ambience of the near Northside Bohemian apartment house,
appear in decline. As in Lonely for the Future, Bailey still aspires to
win Lanson/Raymond to socialism. The one-time socialist candidate for mayor of Cleveland, who spoke side by side with Eugene
Debs in 1912, has been reduced to a wreck with only his faith in
the "sun of socialism" left for comfort.[17] While Bailey is debating
Lanson on the economic basis of theft (as well as almost everything

else), Danny cuts in and declares: "One cause of everything is no cause." [18] Yet, despite his dislike of Bailey's simplicities, the schism separating Danny O'Neill from Ed Lanson's hedonism is far greater by comparison. For example, Danny is visibly repelled by Ed's sneering about the stupidity of humanity and his cynicism about Dreiser's "pity for the people." [19] Danny, like Dreiser, identifies with victimized mankind:

> Dan walked to the window, lit a cigarette and idly stared down on Michigan Avenue below. The people looked small. ... And of course, they were not only diminished in size, but without any of their distinctive, characteristic marks—feature-less. They moved below him as though reduced in their humanity as well as in their size. But they were all men and women and kids, going somewhere, going many places, full of dreams as important to them as his own dreams were to him. Each one was a bundle, a nexus, a collection, an inner organization of pain and sorrow and hopes and dreams; each one of them carried a world of memories; each one of them was living out a destiny as he was.[20]

Danny's empathy for the crushed lives of the masses notwithstanding, his motivation for writing is individual defiance, derived from impulses emergent in *The Silence of History:*

> He wanted to write because it was his only purpose in life, his only justification. He wanted to write because it was the only way he could leave something to stand in the face of death.[21]

Finally Eddie concludes that the most meaningful and enriching art is that predicated on truth at any cost and not on illusion.

Boarding House Blues is set in 1930 and pictures a Danny O'Neill who is progressing, who has an orientation, a fundamental literary and philosophical framework. It portrays (among other things) a young writer who has prepared himself, and who is neither lost nor disoriented by the onslaught of the Depression. He has confidence in himself, in his art, and in certain fundamental ideas. He is moving toward the left, toward socialism, but not by means of sudden revelation or cataclysmic reaction against the past. Rather, his self-reliant radicalism stems from his study of logic and assimilation of experiences.

Farrell himself entered the 1930s in this way, a fighter with a developed arsenal of ideas about life and art and politics. Certainly this was indicated in his 1930 manifesto, "Thirty and Under," where he "attempted to offer a programmatic statement of what I thought writers my age should do and say." [22] The statement accepted responsibility for the new decade; it rejoiced in the fact that "the gathering spirit of the fresh decade is one of affirmation," and that the previous mood of "heartbroken despair," "futility," and "moody skepticism" was being repudiated. Yet there was also a warning:

> A reversion to standards in a period of confusion tempts many into bypaths of misdirection. . . . Looming in the rear of Dr. Babbitt [see footnote 23] is Mother Church. . . .
> The developing positivism of faith has, as yet, not traveled past a series of generalizations, and consequently we are left as confused as ever in the face of many pressing and contemporary problems. All some do is cover a smug retreat from the contemporary situation.

The central question, Farrell emphasized, was that of forging an appropriate response to "the capitalistic, commercial structure of modern life." And in the meanwhile, as long as the social system remained uncontrollably inhumane, the function of art must be one that

> . . . plumbs and explores confusion, chaos, and disorder, to gather a surer comprehenion. Art must tackle experience, not to prove ethical orders and golden proportions, but to derive all the possible meanings that can be deduced.

Although Farrell, like Edmund Wilson and other leftward-moving writers of the time, was attacking the New Humanists, his insistence that literature not be the handmaiden of any formal ideological outlook would instantly make him an object of suspicion when he entered the environs of the Stalinist literary movement. And after that, Farrell would have to defend his stance against censors, against the "League of Frightened Philistines" (Farrell's name for intellectuals he saw as capitulating to wartime hysteria in the 1940s), and against the threatening commercialization of literature.[23]

Several other statements of Farrell in 1930 and 1931 disclosed his orientation at the time. His extensive encounter with the works of Dewey, Mead, James, and Herrick, while only casually mentioned in his fiction, is summed up in his 1930 defense of Dewey against Lewis Mumford's criticism in the *Saturday Review of Literature*. Responding to Mumford's amalgamation of Dewey with the mechanists (who virtually limit themselves to examination of the external environment), Farrell retorted:

> Dr. Dewey's naturalism embraces the concept of existence from which mind emerges. And the emergence of mind, of the power of reflective thought, delimits man's path to freedom and control from the perils of the universe. He would, as C. Judson Herrick does, call mind and reflective thought, natural functions of the human being who exists in a natural situation. This does not disturb the intricacies and subtleties of mental experience; it merely refers them to existence.

Farrell regarded Dewey as being in the vanguard of seekers of a conscious moral and cultural response to problems of modern technological developments, and he closed with a tribute to Dewey as having "the most profound mind yet brought to bear upon the ills of our age."

But Farrell's praise of Dewey included one important political qualification, concerning Dewey's support of World War I:

> There remains a matter of one or two wartime articles in the *New Republic* which constitute a major tragedy in the mental history of our times. . . .[24]

As fiction such as *The Silence of History* reveals, Farrell was strongly affected after the fact by World War I. He deplored the slaughter and was prepared to oppose its repetition. Postwar disillusionment

was an important component of Farrell's revolt in the 1920s, and
he also felt a sense of identification with those who opposed World
War I (such as Randolph Bourne, although he was not uncritical
of Bourne). Furthermore, Farrell was particularly disturbed by the
psychological effects of the war's propagandistic hysteria on the
masses of people, especially young boys incited to day dreams of
going "Over There" to annihilate "The Beasts of Berlin." In the
Studs Lonigan trilogy, the O'Neill-O'Flaherty series, *The Silence of
History,* and other fiction, Farrell subjected such psychological
manipulation (and its gullible acceptance) to ridicule.

With the conviction that "Socialism is inevitable," the belief
that "There will be a second World War" germinated in Farrell in
1926, and both are part of the intellectual awakening in *The Silence
of History:*

> These thoughts took hold of Eddie like illuminations and he
> did not immediately work out the reasons for holding them.
> Yet they rang in his own mind with a conviction of truth, and
> he believed them.[25]

The moral outrage underlying Farrell's antiwar sentiments was
expressed in passages from "Homecoming," a poem written in
1929 and 1930:

> Five flag-draped boxes
> Of rattling bones and odorous flesh
> Were carted away.
> No one remembered,
> No one protested,
> No one asked
> Why they died;
> Not even relatives still proud of their sadness.
> Glory smothered the return
> Of these dead heroes to "their final resting place."
> Glory covered these Archangel casualties,
> These murdered chumps of their country's folly,
> Who came home today,
> Earning with their forgotten lives,
> One day's notice in the *Chicago Herald Examiner.*[26]

This pacifism was a deep-seated conviction of his generation, as the novels of Dos Passos, Hemingway, and others attest.

During the late 1920s and early 1930s Farrell placed numerous book reviews in newspapers in New York and Chicago, as well as in national publications such as the *Nation, Saturday Review of Literature, New Freeman,* and *New Masses.* The range of Farrell's topics is impressive (including poetry, novels, contemporary politics, philosophy, psychology, literary history). A few of these reviews offer insights into Farrell's maturing outlook in the early Depression. For example, in his article, "Plekhanov and Marx," he declared sympathy for Marxism but skepticism about dialectical materialism as a philosophy.[27] The high quality of many of his review articles further indicates a depth of mind, breadth of knowledge, and confident willingness to express critical ideas that distinguished Farrell's growth in that phase. His review of Jane Addams' *The Second Twenty Years at Hull House,* for instance, voiced an admiration for her scientific spirit (which Farrell attributed to John Dewey) while he diplomatically indicated the limitations of a social-work perspective.[28]

Farrell's Paris sojourn in 1931 has not received all the attention it merits, either in his published fiction or in scholarly criticism. Nevertheless, there is no evidence that Parisian events drastically altered Farrell's views; in fact, they seem to have confirmed his direction away from Bohemian aestheticism and toward a humanizing art. In Paris, Farrell continued to work on the Lonigan books, and he finished *Gas-House McGinty* and other fiction. He also read widely, completing all seven volumes of Proust's *Remembrance of Things Past* and Trotsky's *Literature and Revolution.*

Although plagued by financial problems and depressed by the death of his five-day-old son, Sean, Farrell found more avenues for publication in Europe than in the United States.[29] He was also offered support in his literary endeavors by Samuel Putnam and Ezra Pound. But Farrell's friendship with them was tempered by political arguments and disputes. Farrell, having written a critique (highly praised by University of Chicago Professor Harold Laswell) of Por's *Fascism,* was aware of the French fascist *Action Française* and disturbed by Pound's and Putnam's promotion of the Italian fascist movement.[30]

Farrell's statement of intellectual purpose in Peter Neagoe's *Americans Abroad* (1932) recounts the orientation with which he entered the radicalized milieu of New York City in April of 1932:

> I am at present living in France, but belong to no expatriate literary movements, so-called, and am in no sense of the word an expatriate. . . . At present, I am devoting my time almost wholly to fiction, but later I plan to abandon fiction for philosophy. My sympathies are strongly left wing, and I consider most of the things I write to have definite, if implied, points of social criticism.[31]

2.

For New Perspectives

The American writer needs new perspectives. Many felt that the official left wing was giving new perspectives. Now, they are impaled on the falseness of the perspectives given by the official left wing, many can not get off. . . . New perspectives for the American writer must be earned, earned by work, effort, struggle. To gain them, he must gain his own mind, and his own convictions. A new church does not give that, and cannot.

Farrell to Kenneth Patchen, 1937 [1]

Farrell returned to the United States in 1932 with his own notions about philosophy and art, although he proceeded to examine the Communist party's cultural affiliates for new literary perspectives appropriate to the social needs of the Depression decade. Farrell never agreed with or succumbed to the Communist orientation; however, his subsequent debate and controversy with proponents of Stalinist doctrines helped clarify his views. Thus the portraits which seem to emphasize Farrell as a cantankerous

26

trouble-maker in Daniel Aaron's *Writers on the Left*, and as "Peck's bad boy" in Granville Hicks' memoirs, are inadequate.[2] Farrell's literary battles with the Stalinists, which became public in early 1936, largely served as building blocks as he helped construct a conscious literary-political left-wing opposition to the Communists. Even though many aspects of this counter-orientation were not illuminated until Farrell openly linked himself to the Trotskyist current (in late 1936), his criticisms constantly followed the pattern of reaffirming Marxism while repudiating Communist judgments and exhortations. Communist cultural leaders could sense the similarity between this evolution and their previous experiences with Sidney Hook, V. F. Calverton, Herbert Solow, Elliot Cohen, and others. They must have had at least intuitive fears about the course underlying Farrell's literary attacks between 1934 and 1936. Farrell's gravitation toward Trotskyism was ultimately due to a series of political assessments. But the fact that Trotsky also championed a new perspective for writers and artists, at a time when the Communists were in the process of making an embarrassing switch in cultural policy from the sectarian sloganeering of the "Third Period" to the "Popular Front" alliance with commercial and big-name writers of a liberal stamp, was certainly an incentive for Farrell and others to take Trotskyism more seriously.

Farrell moved directly from Paris into the radical literary atmosphere of New York. With his first wife, Dorothy, he stayed at the home of Frances Strauss, then business manager for the *New Masses*. Farrell had first contributed to that magazine back in 1930. The piece was a bitter book review satirizing "American myths" which sanctified the Church, the Boy Scouts, and the flag.[3] Farrell was then unknown, but 1933 saw the publication of *Gas-House McGinty* and 1934 *The Young Manhood of Studs Lonigan*. At the same time Farrell placed a dozen stories in periodicals such as the *American Mercury, Pagany,* and *This Quarter,* as well as nearly a hundred and fifty book reviews (many unsigned) in the *New Republic,* the *New York Post,* the *New York Sun, Scribner's Magazine,* and other publications.

Farrell published his first fiction in the Communist party press at the beginning of 1934: A story in the *Daily Worker* was followed by others in *Partisan Review* (at that time, a John Reed Club organ)

and the *New Masses*.⁴ These stories exemplified Farrell's implied
social criticism and were not specially designed for the Communist
press. Furthermore, an unruly independence marked Farrell's
initial critical contribution to the *New Masses* which made the
article seem to be almost a willful provocation. Farrell participated
in a symposium on Marxist criticism, in which a group of authors
were asked if the *New Masses'* reviews had been helpful. The
respondents included Erskine Caldwell, Robert Cantwell, Jack
Conroy, Josephine Herbst, John Howard Lawson, Edward
Dahlberg, and Farrell. Several of these gave derogatory answers,
but Farrell was noticeably blunt. He simply stated that criticisms
of his works in the *New Masses* had "never raised any challenging
issues that warranted reply." The reasons for this failure, Farrell
maintained, were that the critics lacked an authentic set of
coherent critical principles and were guilty of the "vice of
revolutionary snobbery." Farrell went on to adumbrate ideas
which he would expand two years later into *A Note on Literary
Criticism* (1936). Literary traditions, he said, like scientific principles, were not the property of one class and they required
assimilation by the left. In order to survive, a literary work must
transcend the advocacy of immediate political positions—it must
"assimilate the quality of human worth." Farrell contended that
critical reviews in the *New Masses* had lauded books merely because
of the authors' good political intentions, and the result had been
the praising of rather dreary matter. Farrell declared that this kind
of praise should be excised from the literary criticism section of the
New Masses and relegated to a "Department of Professional
Encouragement." ⁵ Nevertheless, the editors' response to Farrell
was diplomatic. They acknowledged that Farrell was undoubtedly
right in some of his claims, but pointed out that he had failed to
specify the alternatives.⁶

Such diplomacy was consistent with the mixed but generally
favorable reviews that Farrell's books had received regularly in the
New Masses. Writing about *Gas-House McGinty* a year earlier, Edwin
Rolfe praised Farrell's ability to indicate the sources of dissatisfac-
tion in working-class life. These primarily stemmed from the
workers' oppressive job conditions, which regulated and prescribed
their minutest thoughts and activities. Nevertheless, Rolfe an-

nounced, Farrell failed to do more than vaguely indicate the direction in which workers must move to find liberation.[7]

Parallel criticisms appeared in Herman Michaelson's commentary on *Calico Shoes and Other Stories,* published just four months after the 1934 *New Masses* symposium on criticism. Michaelson announced that Farrell was not progressing in his literary work. (The charge really meant that what was not progressing was Farrell's relation to the Communist party.) Farrell's reputation as a writer was "secure in the front rank," Michaelson explained, because of the achievement of the first two Studs Lonigan books (*Young Lonigan* and *The Young Manhood of Studs Lonigan*) and *Gas-House McGinty.* Yet Michaelson believed that in these novels Farrell's own viewpoint was obfuscated: Since his allegiance was to telling the "truth," he showed representative figures from all sides of the class struggle; but he failed to portray the class struggle itself. Farrell dealt with the working class but not the working-class "movement." Michaelson claimed he had heard a report that Farrell planned to publish another Studs Longian book and then lead up to a revolutionary novel by writing twenty-five novels about the life he had experienced; Michaelson warned that if this were true, Farrell's writing would miss "the historical moment," and he would find himself producing works about history after the fact.[8] But Josephine Herbst's 1935 review of *Judgement Day* was virtually free of such recriminations. Her assessment may have been partially due to the fact that the concluding volume of the Studs Lonigan trilogy featured the appearance of a Communist-led parade as the only harbinger of hope for a better world; also, Herbst tended to agree with many of Farrell's literary views, although she loyally subordinated herself to the Stalinists.[9]

Prior to the 1936 declaration of war against Farrell by the leading Stalinist cultural figures, there were two aspects to his relations with the Communist party. Although he published profound criticisms of the party's cultural policy in the *New Masses, Partisan Review,* and the *Nation,* Farrell remained a political collaborator. His book reviews in the *New Masses* were regular features throughout 1935, but most of these were of a neutral character. For example, Farrell satirized Pearl Buck's *A House Divided* for offering a simple-minded plot formula for a best-selling novel. He also criticized Erskine Caldwell's *Journeyman* for, among other things, merely repeating past work, and conveying social implications that were familiar or negligible. From Washington, D.C., Farrell contributed reportage about the attempt of a Louisiana Senator to impede the passage of National Industrial Relations Act legislation by filibustering.[10] But in Farrell's review of *The Valley* by his friend, Nathan Asch (son of the author Sholem Asch), he did offer a criticism applicable to many works by pro-Communist authors: he noted that the endeavor to write "collective novels" (a term then used for books about the way institutions, locales, and groups organize lives) seemed to limit possibilities for character development, which he believed to be a central concern of narrative fiction.[11]

Farrell's modest but significant political collaboration with the Communist party, especially in cultural activities, is recorded in the *Daily Worker*. In January 1935, Farrell's name appeared as one of seventy signers calling for a "Congress of American Revolutionary Writers" on May 1. At the end of April, Farrell was listed as a National Committee member of the newly formed League of American Writers. On May 3, a message from Farrell was included in the *Daily Worker,* with other writers' statements, about the joint Communist-Socialist 1935 May Day parade. Farrell's comment was that the inspiring turnout of the masses showed "who will win the future." Three months later, the *Daily Worker* carried Farrell's highly laudatory review of John L. Spivak's *America Faces the Barricades* (which he declared a "textbook for revolutionary journalism"). In November, Farrell joined with Granville Hicks, Stanley Burnshaw, Hortense Alden (a left-wing actress who would become Farrell's second wife), and the actor Sam Jaffe to form the "Committee to Save *Let Freedom Ring.*" (They urged support for the drama as "one of the finest, truest, most moving labor plays.") [12] On June 27, 1934, the *New Republic* published "An Open Letter to Thomas Mann," endorsed by Farrell and twenty-nine other writers. They demanded that Mann publicly excoriate the oppression of Jews and political dissidents by Nazi Germany.[13]

Farrell also joined a group of writers (including Nathanael West, Herb Kline, and Oakley Johnson) who picketed Ohrbach's Department Store in early 1936 to protest an injunction against the activities of the striking employees. During the demonstration the group crossed Union Square and picketed Klein's store as well. There they were assaulted by mounted police. Edward Newhouse was clubbed, Edward Dahlberg was arrested for violation of the injunction (which was read to him), and the others were indicted for disorderly conduct. One policeman was heard to comment that he failed to understand how "a good Irishman" like Farrell had gotten involved. Farrell spent eight hours in jail and two days in court as a result, although he received a suspended sentence.[14]

Farrell's personal correspondence from the time of his return from Paris until the spring of 1936 confirms this two-sided policy toward the Stalinists: a policy of modest political collaboration balanced by a fundamental antagonism toward their official cultural slogans and standards. In a letter to one of his sisters, shortly after his arrival from France, Farrell urged Mary and her friends to subscribe to the *New Masses*. He also mentioned, irreverently, that he attended a May Day parade and was especially pleased at the absence of long speeches. Most of his correspondence, however, concerned family problems (for example, an upsetting visit with relatives in Chicago) and financial worries.[15]

Farrell's closeness to the Communists and their activities was a more frequent subject in his 1934 correspondence. His letters to Mary—which also solicited factual information for use in writing the O'Neill-O'Flaherty series—mentioned that his Chicago friend, Sam Ross, had become Sports Editor of the *Daily Worker*. Farrell also suggested that when Mary visited New York, she stay with Ed and Rosa Dahlberg, and could receive help in finding a job from Edwin Rolfe at the *Daily Worker*. Comradely letters from Edward Dahlberg during July 1933 denote pleasure about and agreement with Farrell's movement toward Marxism-Leninism.[16]

In letters, Farrell also announced his prospective speech at a *New Masses* symposium in November, and to his friend, Noah Fabricant, he described his work assisting a group of revolutionary poets (including Kenneth Fearing, Edwin Rolfe, and Sol Funaroff, editor of *Dynamo*) in selling their works. Farrell stated that he had spoken on poetry at a New York public meeting to raise money, but that the *"New Masses* Popes" (meaning Alexander Trachtenberg and V.

J. Jerome, the Stalinist overseers of cultural orthodoxy) had seemed cold about the matter.[17] The personal intensity of Farrell's radical political consciousness is evidenced by a passage written to Mary about his immediate family in the spring of 1935:

> As to the Farrells, I agree with most of what you say. And still, well, they are the victims of a system, and the system destroys the decency of many people, it crushes a great number, and as long as the system works it will go on doing that same thing. And they can't see how their own problems are anything more than personal and isolated, and they don't see how they have been educated into slavery to ideas and sentiments which always cause a cleavage between the ways things work out, and the way they are supposed to work out.[18]

At the end of 1935 and the beginning of 1936, Farrell was still dispensing subscriptions to the *New Masses* and soliciting readers for the *Daily Worker* from among relatives. However, in this period references to his controversies with party members and leaders are much more in evidence. All the same, as late as the spring of 1936, Farrell spoke with Communists Josephine Herbst and Granville Hicks at Troy, New York, in defense of a strike in the marble industry.[19]

A salient part of Farrell's maturing critique (or hardening of his early suspicions) of Communist cultural policy evolved outside the pages of the party organs, the *New Masses* and *Daily Worker*. Farrell's first critical disquisition in *Partisan Review,* in an issue containing preparatory discussion for the 1935 Writers' Congress, was almost an indictment. Edwin Seaver offered the lead article called, "What is a Proletarian Novel?" Responses by Edwin Burgum, Henry Hart, and Farrell also were printed. It is worthwhile to contrast the views.

Seaver pointed to the paradox that authentic workers could write nonproletarian works, while middle-class writers could compose on a petit bourgeois subject which could qualify as being from a "proletarian" view. Seaver suggested that the means for judging literature were bound up in the political character of the period in which the work was written. The proletarian novelist is

one, Seaver concluded, whose class alignment is with the proletariat and whose ideological approach to story and characters
corresponds to the Marxist interpretation of the historical process:
"And not only the acceptance, but the use of this interpretation [is
required] as a compelling factor in his work." [20]

Burgum and Hart endorsed Seaver's analysis. The former
offered a crude system for classifying types of bourgeois novels, and
Hart recommended that the label "revolutionary novel" might be
used for works which were ideologically Marxist, but without a
proletarian subject matter. In contrast, Farrell, without remarking
on Seaver's article directly, contended that Communist critics were
creating a new scholasticism, applying labels to and making
judgments about literature for extraliterary purposes, as a substitute for assimilating and employing the knowledge of past
literary traditions. Farrell's was the only rejoinder directly to cite
works and views of Marx and Engels, and he explicitly utilized this
material to refute what he believed was ersatz "Marxist criticism."
In this respect, Farrell's approach was quite similar to that of two
of *Partisan Review*'s editors, William Phillips and Philip Rahv. They
also opposed extraliterary tests of excellence in the cultural left by
using arguments from Marx and Lenin. The more famous Farrell,
however, was franker and less diplomatic in his criticisms.

Farrell's overall contribution to *Partisan Review,* in its Communist
party period between 1934 and 1936 as well as after its transformation into an organ of literary anti-Stalinism (late in 1937), was
considerable. Farrell was not an initiator of the journal, but he
circulated in the milieu of its supporters. (For example, Farrell was
present at an early planning meeting which occurred while he was
staying at Edward Dahlberg's house in the beginning of 1935.)
Phillips and Rahv approached Farrell for contributions when
Partisan Review first began. Farrell induced Josephine Herbst and
Horace Gregory to submit material and helped raise money for the
enterprise. One evening in August 1935 Phillips and Rahv met
Farrell on 8th Street and asked him to write a piece called "Farrell
on Faulkner" (to which he agreed, although the article never
materialized). That fall, they, along with Alan Calmer (another
editor of the original *Partisan Review*), visited Farrell at his
Lexington Avenue and 29th Street apartment to request that he

contribute a regular theater column. During this interval, Phillips and Rahv also confided to Farrell that efforts were being made by Granville Hicks, Malcolm Cowley, Alexander Trachtenberg, and other Communist cultural leaders to abolish the maverick journal.[21]

The first of Farrell's five installments in the "Theatre Chronicle" department of *Partisan Review* (later to be the province of Mary McCarthy when the magazine was reorganized) was his most memorable. There, in early 1936, Farrell made fun of the excessive praise heaped on the left-wing playwright Clifford Odets, whom Communist critics had compared to Chekhov, O'Casey, O'Neill, Tolstoy, Dreiser, and Wolfe. Farrell countered with a balanced criticism of the strengths and weaknesses of the three works on which Odets' reputation was based and then humorously demolished Odets' latest work, *Paradise Lost.* Farrell dubbed the play a "burlesque" of Odets' previous work, such as *Awake and Sing,* and suggested it be retitled "Lay Down and Die." [22] For the most part, Farrell's Theatre Chronicle column remained highly censorious of current American drama (and left-wing plays especially), with Maxwell Anderson's *Winterset* and Sidney Kingsley's *Dead End* coming under harsh assault.

Farrell's irreverent article on Odets ended all pretense of diplomacy by the Stalinist cultural leadership. Their antagonism had increased prior to the Odets review, especially because of Farrell's critical expositions of Communist party cultural policy (including his address made in 1935 to the American Writers' Congress on the short story), [23] and his animadversions on "proletarian" novels in reviews for the non-Communist press. This last incursion had included skeptical considerations of Jack Conroy's *The Disinherited,* Robert Cantwell's *The Land of Plenty,* Clara Weatherwax's *Marching! Marching!,* and Robert Briffault's *Europa.*

Farrell's commentary on Conroy's *The Disinherited* in the *Nation* in late 1933 had been a particular source of irritation to the Stalinists. Although Farrell had moderately praised the novel for realistic reportage and the use of an authentic American idiom, he also used it to discourse against the temptation to sacrifice depth of characterization and technical proficiency in the interest of mere local color. To highlight Conroy's failings, Farrell counterposed Russian writers who had also depicted individuals living in poverty: "But their characters were human beings who experienced every human emotion, who had, if an antiquated word be permissible, 'souls.' " [24]

Despite the famous quarrel that ensued, there is no evidence that Farrell sought to launch any momentous attack against Conroy, whom he had never met (although Farrell had heard Conroy's name mentioned and seen his stories published in the *American Mercury*). In truth, Farrell originally submitted a brief note on Conroy to the *Nation*, but literary editor Margaret Marshall returned it and requested a lengthier consideration. Soon after publication of the review, Farrell heard stories that Conroy was writing letters complaining about and attacking him.[25]

Only a short time later, in February 1934, Edward Dahlberg reviewed *The Young Manhood of Studs Lonigan* in the *New Masses*. There he criticized Conroy's prose as simply "rehash," and praised Farrell's as "skillfully and deeply fused." [26] Although Farrell had not encouraged Dahlberg in this enterprise, the two were known to be good friends. The resulting resentment of some Conroy partisans was probably reflected in a letter from Henry George Weiss to the *New Masses* the following April.[27] Weiss deplored the fact that Dahlberg's article had elevated the writing of Farrell above that of Conroy. Farrell, Weiss argued, simply borrowed Joyce's techniques and wrote of the age-old theme of the degradation of the poor. Conroy, however, must be acknowledged a pioneer of the proletarian novel. He was a writer whose work would live longer because it treated "the vital affirmative class." [28] Such comments were symptomatic of a small movement of Conroy fans. Farrell recalled:

Conroy influenced a number of young left writers, in the Middle West, to attack me in conversation, etc. They were a kind of anti-Farrell gallery.

When Conroy came to the American Writers' Congress in New York, in 1935, it seemed that a Conroy-Farrell feud had grown up out of this. I did poke some fun at him at the

Congress, and I spoke at one meeting, on fiction, and while a
bit drunk, breaking up the meeting more or less, and trying to
get Conroy or any of his Mid-Western friends to say
something.

He and his friends went on attacking me whenever they could.
In the thirties, once or twice, one of them sent me collect
telegrams of an insulting nature.[29]

In an interview thirty years later, Conroy declared that he
believed Farrell's review of *The Disinherited* to be "unfairly carp-
ing." [30] Elsewhere he claimed that Farrell had found his rural
origin an excuse for heavy-handed humor on several occasions and
had dubbed him "Jack Cornrow" at the First American Writers'
Congress.[31] The actual record of the dispute between Farrell and
Conroy, however, seems to go beyond the limits of a mere personal
squabble; it probably never would have been sanctioned by
Conroy's pro-Stalinist supporters if they desired a serious hearing
for Farrell's views and the preservation of his literary stature. (It
should be noted, however, that Conroy believes that the Communists' reasons for objecting to Farrell were not the same as his.) [32]
But the dispute is worth tracing, as a representative altercation
between Farrell and pro-Communist elements.

In late 1937, the pages of the *New Republic* contained a plethora
of assaults on Farrell. First, there was a hostile review of *The Short
Stories of James T. Farrell* by Otis Ferguson. Then a letter from Jack
Conroy praised this condemnation as a "monumental piece" only
"much too mild." Next, there was a letter signed by twenty-six
names (many fictitious) from East St. Louis, calling Farrell a
"pretentious windbag" and a "palpable fraud." In reply, two
letters of objection were printed: one, from F. W. Dupee, called the
anti-Farrell campaign a "pogrom"; the other, from Dwight
Macdonald, protested the "childish" and "malicious" instance of a
"literary lynching." [33] (Macdonald and Dupee were by this time
on the editorial board of the new *Partisan Review*.) A letter sent to
Farrell by Robert Morss Lovett in 1944 implicated Malcolm
Cowley as supportive of Conroy in beleaguering Farrell. Lovett

also deplored the animosity which the *New Republic* had displayed toward Farrell's work as a rule.[34]

Conroy was still carrying on his part in the quarrel in the mid-1960s and early 1970s. He spiced his contribution to the *Carleton Miscellany* symposium on "The Thirties" with a blast at Murray Kempton's laudatory portrait of Farrell in *Part of Our Time*.[35] And in his 1973 introduction to *Writers in Revolt: The Anvil Anthology*, Conroy records that fundraising activities for relaunching the magazine *Anvil* in the late 1930s included the following:

> More money was raised from the staging in several Chicago locations of *The Drunkard's Warning, or Chicago by Gaslight*. This melodrama was the tear-jerking tale of James T. Barrelhouse, "a minor trilogist and puissant polemicist" whose enslavement to strong waters had not only made a sodden wreck of him but had blighted the lives of his noble wife Phyllis and their small daughter Lily.[36]

But the attacks by Conroy, and those which appeared in the *New Republic,* were only a continuation of the public denunciations of Farrell that had been initiated in February of 1936 by the Communist writer Mike Gold. Incited by Farrell's debunking of Clifford Odets' *Paradise Lost* in the *Partisan Review,* a journal of which the Communists were already suspicious, Gold censured Farrell in an article written allegedly to "celebrate" the merging of *Partisan Review* and *Anvil* into one literary journal. Without naming names, Gold commenced with a few barbs directed at the New York intellectual critics associated with the former *Partisan Review,* imputing to them a "terrible mandarinism":

> They carry their Marxian scholarship as though it were a heavy cross. They perform academic autopsies on living books. They wax pious and often sectarian. Often, they use a scholastic jargon as barbarous as the terminology that for so long infected most Marxian journalism in this country, a foreign language no American could understand without a year or two of post-graduate study.

But this was only a prelude to Gold's real object of attack. The Stalinist cultural leader accused Farrell of having a "prejudice" against Clifford Odets, reminiscent of "the stale old Bohemian days of the literary feuds." Gold continued:

> When one remembers that Farrell also attacked Jack Conroy's first novel, *The Disinherited,* saying in the *Nation,* that the book had "no soul" (this from the author of the most soulless novels in recent America); and that Farrell wrote a sour review of Clara Weatherwax's fine novel in the *Herald-Tribune,* one begins to wonder what is wrong, and whether Farrell has the objectivity and generosity—let us also add sense—to be a critic.[37]

According to Farrell's recollection, a number of writers associated with the *New Masses* planned to submit a protest letter defending him against the attack. But the Communist cultural leaders, up in arms about an alleged "Farrell faction," succeeded in quieting most of them. The end result was the publication of a softened version of a letter critical of Gold which Josephine Herbst had written to the *New Masses.* It was printed in the Communist journal, but followed by an answer from Gold.[38] The bowdlerized letter from Herbst stated that Gold's disquisition on the new *Partisan Review and Anvil* venture was simply an excuse for him to attack Farrell. She asserted that Gold's "anti-intellectualism" had been bothering her for a long time, and that it was Gold who showed prejudice when he dismissed Farrell's books *in toto* as "soulless." It was Herbst's opinion that Farrell possessed "evident intellectual integrity and achievements," and she doubted that it was possible to construct a left-wing literary "united front" when Gold was so "inhospitable to professional writers drawn to the left." She emphasized that because Gold possessed an imposing position in the Communist movement he was obliged to be especially cautious and diplomatic in his literary judgments.[39]

In answering Herbst, Gold insisted that the Communist party never authorized an official pontificator of literary verdicts. He declared that his object had not been to attack Farrell but simply to defend Odets, whom Farrell had allegedly slighted with personal obloquy even before discussing *Paradise Lost.* But Gold confirmed that he felt "more at home" with the likes of Jack Conroy than with Farrell.[40]

Farrell never retorted directly to the *New Masses* on this matter, but his views were argued in the sections of his work in progress, *A Note on Literary Criticism,* which were already appearing in the *Nation.*[41] Additionally, Farrell's review of Granville Hicks' *The Great Traditon* was published a few weeks later in the *American Spectator* with the editor's title, "Mr. Hicks: Critical Vulgarian."[42] Besides, Farrell continued several more installments of the "Theatre Chronicle" in *Partisan Review,* and at least some of his comments were aimed at the dispute:

> Criticism and reviewing should be, primarily, the means of judgment, interpretation, and evaluation. If the critic or the reviewer sacrifices this function in order to become an agent of professional encouragement, he will quickly become indistinguishable from many of the bourgeois critics whom he professes to despise.[43]

Farrell's private correspondence also evidences the accumulating tensions between himself and the Stalinists which exploded in public controversy and reached its apex when *A Note on Literary Criticism* appeared on May 20, 1936. A February letter from Farrell to novelist Robert Cantwell argued against praising a critic simply because a certain method was employed; one must also evaluate *how* the critical method was employed.[44] Letters to Farrell's sister Mary tell of the attacks by Gold and the progress of his book on literary criticism.[45] Writing to his brother Jack, who at that time felt some sympathy for the Stalinists, Farrell subjected the Communist cultural movement to a scathing indictment:

> the united front in the cultural and literary wing has reached the limit beyond which it is not even an absurdity.

Farrell described a membership meeting of the League of American Writers (which he referred to as "The League Against American Writing"). Desiring to implement the new course of the

Popular Front, Malcolm Cowley, John Howard Lawson, and others considered scheduling the next national gathering so as not to interfere with the vacation plans of noted literary figures (such as Ernest Hemingway and Sinclair Lewis). They also argued the urgency of using moderate nonradical language so as not to frighten off desired liberal participants like Henry Seidel Canby and Fannie Hurst:

> Do you [Farrell wrote Jack] want any clearer or more decisive answer to your suggestions . . . about my getting closer? My name was suggested as one to be added to the committee planning this conference, If I am invited—most likely they will veto me on the grounds that I am a disruptive influence— do you think that I intend to sit around and listen to all that junk, and not get up and talk plainly? And if I do that, how can I draw closer? I shall be thrown out on my can. . . .[46]

A Note on Literary Criticism evolved from a short essay expressing ideas which had been fermenting in Farrell's mind for about four years (although the book itself was rewritten three times and assembled in one month).[47] Even though it concerned problems of the current left-wing dispute, a distinctive feature of *A Note on Literary Criticism* was how logically its Marxist, Leninist, and Trotskyist ideas and arguments seemed to flow from the fount of Farrell's thought in the late 1920s. The short critical book (221 pages) seemed a wholly consistent outgrowth of Farrell's ideas as formulated before he had entered the thick of the New York radical milieu, and before he had read Trotsky's *Literature and Revolution* in 1932. The arguments were a Marxist extension of that prior intellectual development, and the book's central formulation (distinguishing the aesthetic and functional aspects of art) was directly inspired by Mead and Dewey.

Written in a straightforward personal style, *A Note on Literary Criticism* was nevertheless scholarly and thorough, as Farrell systematically refuted the most common critical fallacies of Stalinist dogma. Not a leading American Communist figure was left untouched. Farrell exposed Gold (as a revolutionary sentimentalist), Hicks (as a mechanical determinist), Seaver, Cowley, the early Rahv, and even V. F. Calverton (who had himself been at loggerheads with the Stalinists since 1933). In several areas of *A Note on Literary Criticism* there were also signs of a parallel with the simultaneously developing orientation of the Phillips-Rahv wing of the old *Partisan Review:* particularly in Farrell's acknowledgment of the necessity of assimilating literary tradition; his opposition to manifestations of "leftism" (meaning a sectarian, pedantic, and mechanical Marxism); his aspiration to incorporate technical innovations from the 1920s (especially those of Joyce, whom Farrell defended against scurrilous abuse in writings by Karl Radek and the Stalinist Dmitri Mirsky). Farrell quoted abundantly from texts and correspondence of Marx, Engels, and Lenin (Plekhanov, however, was excluded); but he was careful not to argue that such authority proved anything in itself. In a characteristic formulation, Farrell remarked that " . . . the theory of the relative objective validity of art" is "not inconsistent with Marxism as a body of thought and a method of analysis." [48]

The book mentioned neither Stalin nor Trotsky, although the latter's *Literature and Revolution* was clearly echoed when Farrell polemicized against premature declarations of the existence of "proletarian" or "socialist" culture:

> We know [wrote Farrell] that through the Russian Revolution and the establishment of the USSR, this movement [toward socialism] has, during the last eighteen years, been given a tremendous impetus. We know that with the extension of the world revolution it will create a new Socialist Society. Socialism will slowly, gradually, permeate every sphere of human activity; will be correspondingly felt in thought, in literature, in the drama, in all the cultural spheres that compose the Socialist superstructure. But this change is not going to be brought about by fiat; it will not come merely from our wishing, nor through stout assertion that it is already here. . . . The new culture that will grow from a new society will not precede that society, for thought and culture do not precede social changes: at best they guide toward such changes.[49]

The critical reception of *A Note on Literary Criticism* probably could have been predicted. The *Partisan Review* gave it a favorable notice, written by Alan Calmer; Edmund Wilson praised it highly in the *Nation;* and the *New Masses* arraigned it severely. Writing in the *New Masses,* Isador Schneider asserted that what *A Note on Literary Criticism* represented was not at all the work of a single malcontent but the reflection of a group or current of thought on the cultural left. *A Note on Literary Criticism,* Schneider announced, was "an indication of a new crisis in revolutionary literature." Schneider's article acknowledged the correctness of a number of Farrell's recriminations against sectarian aberrations of the left. This was not conceded by Schneider simply because of the cogency of Farrell's arguments: in truth, Farrell's book was harassing the Stalinists at an awkward time, for the implementation of their Popular Front orientation was already under way. Schneider could hardly leap to the defense of the very past policies (namely, the super-revolutionary sloganeering of the Third Period) which the Stalinists were hastening to shove under the rug.

Thus, Schneider's only defense could be that past "excesses" were justified in a certain stage of the earlier 1930s and that Farrell's methodological weakness lay precisely in his inability to comprehend that different situations demanded shifts in cultural tactics. Schneider leaped to the slanderous conclusion that because Farrell had catalogued so many left-wing critical catastrophes, his "real" argument was "that Marxist criticism in America had failed, and should quickly be put away and forgotten." Schneider attributed to Farrell the position of opposing "Marxist criticism" although Farrell had claimed that his actual revulsion was against Communist caricatures of Marxist criticism. Schneider ended with the explanation that the new Popular Front policies of the Comintern necessitated a complete turn from previous "proletarian cultural" concepts, but that Farrell's book represented an overreaction:

> Dimitrov, in his analysis of the general program of the united [Popular] front, warned against the political dangers of the swing to the right, of the dissolution of revolutionary principles. The appearance of Farrell's book indicates that the

danger also exists in the literary field. Certainly, the fact that the Catholic Book Club recommends *A Note on Literary Criticism* illuminates the nature of its Marxism.[50]

The following week the *New Masses* printed a letter from Schneider stating that, because he had received so many complaints about the reference to the Catholic Book Club in his review's last paragraph, a clarification was necessary: He was *not* claiming that Farrell supported the Catholic Church, but simply that it was "indicative" that the Catholic Church found Farrell's book agreeable.[51]

Although the *New Masses* printed nothing on the controversy for several weeks, the obvious impact of Farrell's book and the inadequacy of Schneider's article in coping with the "crisis" were exposed by the appearance of a second *New Masses* review of *A Note on Literary Criticism*—this time by Granville Hicks. Ironically titled "In Defense of James T. Farrell," Hicks' article took a strangely different approach from that of Schneider. Whereas Schneider had praised the quality of much of Farrell's work and arguments, he had also described them as expressing a new tendency which would ultimately lead to the liquidation of Marxism. Hicks, in contrast, proclaimed the following: (1) the book was in fact barren of ideas and original argument; (2) it was, however, essentially Marxist, despite the fact that Farrell *himself* was retreating from Marxism and blinded by his grudges against leading left writers.[52]

Four contributions sparked by the controversial impact of *A Note on Literary Criticism* appeared in the August 18 *New Masses*. First, Farrell published a rebuttal in which he pointed to an inconsistency in the fact that Schneider had agreed with so many of his conclusions, yet he denounced almost all of his fundamental premises. Farrell shrewdly underscored the point that when he had criticized the *New Masses'* sentimentalism and mechanical determinism, it was because of disagreements on the fundamental issue of the social influence of literature. Schneider, in contrast, could only perceive such issues as questions of the legislation of literary tactics (for example, at one time sectarianism was required, Schneider would say, but now it is not). Furthermore, Farrell refuted the charge that his book challenged whether or not "there is any function for Marxist criticism." What he had asked, Farrell clarified, was whether there was any function for the *abuses* of Marxism such as those found in the "revolutionary sentimentality" of Gold and the "mechanical materialism" of Hicks.[53]

Following Farrell's rebuttal came a weak reply by Schneider in which he adopted Hicks' line of argument. Schneider now stated that Farrell's critical principles were Marxist, but that Farrell had distorted the views of others (such as Gold and Hicks) by quoting "tactical works" out of context. A letter from Sidney Siegel, the third item, endorsed Farrell's views while deploring Schneider's abuse of "dialectics" to justify past errors. Following this came an indignant letter from Morris U. Schappes which attempted to pinpoint Farrell's alleged falsifications in regard to Hicks' *The Great Tradition.* (Farrell answered Schappes several issues later, and Schappes responded again at the end of September.) [54] Thus ended the controversy around *A Note on Literary Criticism* in the Stalinist camp.

Two reviews by important members of the anti-Stalinist left are also worth noting. The most rewarding response to *A Note on Literary Criticism* was Edmund Wilson's commendation in the *Nation.*[55] Especially in view of the hostile reaction from the pro-Communists, it seemed "worth publishing the polemic in order to have received such a tribute from our best critic," wrote the Trotskyist George Novack to Farrell in early July 1936.[56] The second review, which raises some useful issues that can serve as a transition to discussing Farrell's increasing ties with Trotskyism, was a two-part exposition by V. F. Calverton in *Modern Monthly.*[57]

V. F. Calverton (whose real name was George Goetz) was a prolific writer and editor who had at one time been close to the Communist party. By the mid-1930s, however, he was an avowed anti-Stalinist and had already been subject to calumny and verbal abuse by the party for several years. Yet some of his remarks on Farrell were strangely unsympathetic. He did hail Farrell as a "striking creative artist" who could exercise "independence of judgment," but Calverton also claimed that in *A Note on Literary Criticism* Farrell was merely "educating himself in public." Calverton maintained that Farrell's arguments largely repeated platitudes of Marxist aesthetics which had already been endorsed even

FOR NEW PERSPECTIVES   45

by the critics identified with the Communist party. Since Calverton was the author of several books and many articles on literature
and society, part of his censure of Farrell's work may have sprung
from a desire to defend his own position of being the authoritative
spokesman in this area (especially since Farrell was a potential
competitor of considerable prestige).[58] One part of Calverton's
critique, however, was indubitably correct: Farrell had approached
the nature and function of Stalinism as a social movement only by
implication. *A Note on Literary Criticism* appeared to be an arraignment of individual stupidities of the critics identified with the
Communist party; it did not systematize and expose the errors as
manifestations of the subordination of cultural judgments to
sectarian political exigencies of the Soviet political regime. Why,
demanded Calverton, had Farrell not even mentioned Trotsky's
Literature and Revolution, which was "the most brilliant book" on the
subject? (To further emphasize this omission, Calverton even
entitled the second installment of his article, "James T. Farrell and
Leon Trotsky.")

In order to answer this question, one must recognize that Farrell
was not simply breaking with Stalinism on an individual level, but
that he had set his goal as reorienting the literary left in a new,
revolutionary socialist direction. In other words, Calverton was
inaccurate when he declared that Farrell's refusal to be explicit
about the issues in the Communist International's internecine
political warfare was evidence that Farrell himself wished to
remain in the "safe domain of the cultural front." Farrell's decision
to omit direct mention of the Trotsky controversy was a tactical
choice made because he wanted "to nail the Stalinists and not give
them an opportunity to divert from the real dispute." [59]

This strategy had not been worked out in isolation. In the
summer of 1934, at the artists' and writers' colony of Yaddo in
Saratoga Springs, New York, Farrell was completing *Judgment
Day;* [60] there he came to know George Novack. Novack was then a
young executive in the publishing industry, who circulated in left-
wing intellectual circles that included Sidney Hook and individuals from the former *Menorah Journal* group, some of whom had
moved toward Trotskyism. In 1936, Novack read the manuscript of
A Note on Literary Criticism before it was published; together Farrell

and Novack discussed the tactics with which it should be presented. In Novack's view, the line of the book was consistent with and partially inspired by Trotsky's *Literature and Revolution*. Novack believed that at that point Farrell had already broken with Stalinist politics inwardly, although he had not yet done so publicly.[61] The association of Novack with Farrell is central for an understanding of the latter's involvement with Trotskyism and merits a separate chapter.

3.

James T. Farrell
and George Novack in the 1930s

As a Harvard student I was at first interested in aesthetic values, and for a while I was overwhelmed by Nietzsche. But then I began to feel the grip of *The Education of Henry Adams* upon me: Adams and his brother, Brooks, had sought the laws of historical development. After a memorable discussion with one of my classmates about that search, I concluded that if one could find out the laws governing the destiny of mankind, this would be a powerful instrument to predict the future. After the 1929 Crash, this preoccupation led me directly toward Marxism.

George Novack, 1973 [1]

George Edward Novack was born in Boston in 1905, of Jewish immigrants from eastern Europe. His maternal grandmother, who never learned English, owned a grocery store in the West End. Neither of his parents advanced in education beyond grammar school, and his father worked as a newsboy and a teamster, before becoming an agent for John Hancock Life Insurance and a professional gambler. The family had transferred from the West End tenement district to Somerville, a lower-middle-class area of suburban Boston, where Novack was raised. After Novack attended high school, the family moved to Brookline.

Possessed of an intellectual bent from childhood, Novack matriculated at Harvard in 1922. His initial inclination was toward English literature, but he soon turned to philosophy. He aspired to write, and the philosophy of history became his chief interest. With the exception of this absorbing concern, most of Novack's other preoccupations were typical of the period and the milieu. Apart from the students' literary vanguardism and sexual experimentation, the Harvard environment was a politically conservative one during the years Novack attended, from 1922 to 1927. He participated actively in the social and fraternity life of the Jewish liberal intellectuals, and read T. S. Eliot, Marcel Proust, Virginia Woolf, James Joyce, and W. B. Yeats.

Novack never graduated from Harvard, although he passed five years there and managed to quit three times. He recollected that he spent many hours in Widener Library, reading philosophy from one end of the shelf to the other. Novack also studied with the main figures in the Harvard Philosophy Department: C. I. Lewis and Ralph Perry. He took classes with Alfred North Whitehead, who was then writing *Process and Reality,* chapters of which he read aloud to Novack's class.

The Harvard campus was politically shaken only twice during that decade: at the time of the Sacco-Vanzetti execution and when H. L. Mencken was arrested for selling a banned issue of *American Mercury* on Boston Common. Although Novack had a wide acquaintance in left-liberal circles at Harvard, Marxism, about which he knew nothing, never appeared to him as an option. He recalled that there was a small socialist club of eight to ten members and no Communists of whom he was aware.

In late 1927, Novack moved to New York City, where he worked for a lecture bureau and then Doubleday and Company at Garden City, Long Island. In 1929, he became Advertising Manager for E. P. Dutton, which had one of the biggest advertising budgets in the business. He remained there until 1934. Novack was able to write as part of his job, where he also learned discipline in technical matters. Although he aspired to write a book on philosophy, he had difficulty finding his bearings; his only publication, prior to becoming a Trotskyist, was a book of wisecracks edited with Arthur Zipser called *Who's Hooey* (1932). Radicalized by the Crash of 1929, Novack recalled that he began to study assiduously and that he began learning the Marxist method in 1931.

Novack maintained his friendships with college associates who lived in New York and made the acquaintance of similar liberal intellectuals who had recently left their campuses and were initiating professional careers. He married Elinor Rice, a former Barnard student who ran a 44th Street bookstore. Through her friendship with Diana (Rubin) Trilling, Novack became a part of the circle which had originally been linked to the *Menorah Journal.*

In the 1930s, George Novack attempted to blend his paramount preoccupations, history and philosophy, through Marxism. Starting in 1932, Novack pursued his intellectual course while also participating in the National Committée for the Defense of Political Prisoners (an intellectuals' adjunct to the Communist International Labor Defense). He became head of the Political Prisoners Book Committee, which sent publications to the McNamara Brothers, Warren Billings, Tom Mooney, and others.

In December 1933, Novack was included in "an informally organized revolutionary club" initiated by Sidney Hook. Also involved were Lewis Corey, George S. Counts, Meyer Schapiro, Felix Morrow, James Burnham, Reinhold Niebuhr, Herbert Solow, Louis Hacker, Max Lerner, Corliss Lamont, and Waldo Frank.[2] After joining the Communist League of America (Trotskyist) in the fall of 1933, Novack devoted part of his intellectual interests to the work of another, overlapping group of radical historians. These young scholars aspired to transcend what they believed to be the shortcomings of liberal historians such as Charles Beard and Vernon Parrington. A number of them belonged to the Historical Project of the Works Progress Administration, located in the New York Public Library. Officially, the Project was largely bibliographical and involved a study of American historical literature. Louis Hacker was the head of it, as well as the inspiring figure. Associated with the work were other anti-Stalinist radicals, like Lewis Corey, and Trotskyists such as Herbert Solow, Felix Morrow, and John McDonald.

Novack sympathized with what he believed was their unofficial goal of reinterpreting American history along Marxist lines, studying it from below—from the standpoint of workers and the common people. Attempting to avoid a sentimental or Populist thrust, they looked to the historical writings of Marx and Trotsky as models. Members of the group produced some scholarly works, but in the opinion of Novack the ultimate goal was never realized.[3] During this interval, Novack was more engrossed in American history than philosophy. He finished the first part of a projected three-volume study which presented the Civil War as the second and concluding stage of the bourgeois-democratic revolution in the United States.[4]

When Novack and Farrell met at Yaddo in the summer of 1934, Novack found himself "the lone oppositionist amidst thirteen Communist members or sympathizers."[5] But Farrell had been interested in Trotsky before meeting Novack. He had read *Literature and Revolution* in Paris and some of Trotsky's articles. In these earlier years, Trotsky had impressed Farrell as primarily a romantic figure. Then at Yaddo, Farrell read Max Eastman's translation of *The History of the Russian Revolution* for the first time and was impressed by it.

The friendship between Novack and Farrell was not the only or most important factor in Farrell's political unfolding. But Novack (along with Felix Morrow and James Burnham) was one of the most important of the New York intellectuals who stayed with the Trotskyists for any length of time; therefore, the record of Novack's decade-long friendship with Farrell, documented by correspondence, is one salient indicator of the bonds which linked Farrell to the Trotskyist movement.

From the beginning, the correspondence between Novack and Farrell affirmed that the literary ideas professed by Novack were consistent with those of Farrell: Both were united against the official Stalinist cultural leadership. In November, following their Yaddo acquaintance, Novack praised Farrell's *Calico Shoes and Other Stories* because, "with all their peculiarities as individuals, the people you create are native to their environment, cultural as well as social and local." Novack then proceeded to outline a literary perspective markedly similar to that which Farrell had already formed, and which Farrell would develop in his coming battles with literary Stalinism:

> ... by indirection [Novack wrote] your work does serve a revolutionary purpose. And that's the way I conceive an artist's work should affect people. Not by taking them by direct assault, but by sapping the foundations of their beliefs. This fact strikes me freshly because this week I've vainly tried to read Josephine Herbst's new book, *The Executioner Waits*. Here is a prize example of what the John Reed Club thinks a novel by a "proletarian" writer should be—and the result, so far as I could read, which was not far, is a stillborn opus which hadn't a breath of life in it. The book doesn't come out of her life or the life of active human beings, but out of a set of notions floating around in her head. She's nothing but a manufacturer of fiction for a particular class of consumers with low literary standards.[6]

Novack's disposition toward Farrell's fiction was further developed in a 1936 critical discussion of *A World I Never Made*. There Novack illuminated Farrell's project with Trotsky's comments in the beginning of *My Life*. Trotsky had noted that the idealization of happy childhood had "originated in the old literature of the privileged," and constituted an "aristocratic view":

> But the majority of the people [wrote Trotsky], if it looks back at all, sees, on the contrary, a childhood of darkness, hunger, and dependence. Life strikes the weak—and who is weaker than a child?

Novack did criticize Farrell's portrayal of the business rivals, Robinson and Brophy, suggesting that they seemed "cardboard." This stemmed, Novack believed, from Farrell's lack of "sympathy, knowledge, and insight" into that type of person. However, Novack praised Farrell's depiction of the family life and environmental forces shaping the child, Danny O'Neill, as well as the growth in stature of the "authentic" but unidealized proletarian, Jim O'Neill. Novack commended Farrell's

> . . . keen eye for the most minute gradations in the social scale and for the habits of social intercourse which grow out of them. In dealing with these two interpenetrating strata of urban existence, the lower middle class milieu which touches at various points the superior realms of gold and government above and merges almost imperceptively with the proletariat in the slums below, he presents not a pretty picture but a real one.

Novack declared:

> This novel together with the Lonigan trilogy, marks out Farrell as the most promising and productive of the younger novelists who are writing in the Dreiserian tradition of urban realism, the sturdiest tradition in modern literature, simply because the metropolis is the central power station of our times.[7]

The literary compatibility between the urban realist Farrell and the Trotskyist Novack was not a central bond; rather, it served to facilitate the relationship. Certainly it removed one obstacle that might have distanced Farrell from the political ideas of Trotskyism. Throughout the 1930s Novack wrote Farrell frequently. He often discussed central issues of the day from the Trotskyist perspective. For example, in an undated letter (probably written in late 1934), Novack attempted to reply to some basic questions directed to him by Farrell:

> Your doubts about Trotsky seem understandable but unfounded. First, could any man be right so often? History supplies the answer and Trotsky's writings before the events confirm it. 1905, 1917, and 1933 were triumphant tests for Trotsky's predictions and analyses of events, although only one was a triumph for the proletariat. Not that Trotsky was

infallible. He is not a superman, incapable of error, as for example Ralph Fox makes Lenin out to be in his systematically falsified life of Lenin. He was wrong in his "conciliationism" between the Mensheviks, Bolsheviks, and Social Revolutionaries in the period between 1905 and 1912 and Lenin right. He admits it. He was also wrong and Lenin right in the trade-union question after the October Revolution. But at the crucial hour on the decisive questions he and Lenin stood side by side and saw eye to eye. This simply to get the historical record straight.[8]

The following spring, 1935, Elizabeth Ames, director of Yaddo, invited Novack to return, and Farrell may have encouraged her to make the invitation.[9] In any event, Farrell wrote Ames the next year, 1936, urging that Novack be invited back a third time. He commented that Novack had a "good mind" and needed a chance "to get away from passing journalism and into theoretical stuff—history of American philosophy and social thought." [10]

Novack's letters to Farrell during 1936 contained lengthy political elaborations and even translations of news analysis from the French Trotskyist press. The primary events observed were the 1936 summer strike wave in France, the Civil War in Spain, and the 1936 American presidential elections.[11]

Farrell's unpublished diary for the year 1936 records the continuation of his intensive study of Marxist politics. In late April Farrell read Earl Browder's *What is Communism?* and found it disappointing.[12] In early July Farrell recorded a conversation held with Joseph Freeman,[13] and completed Trotsky's *The Third International After Lenin*. He said he was making up his mind about the important questions of the international communist dispute.[14] Besides these books, Farrell's list of completed readings for the year 1936 included Trotsky's *Communism and Terrorism, Whither France?*, and *Literature and Revolution*, and two important works by American Trotskyists: Max Shachtman's *Behind the Moscow Trials* and Felix Morrow's pamphlet, *The Civil War in Spain*.[15]

Furthermore, the diary chronicles Farrell's efforts in urging other radical intellectuals to break with the Stalinists. By August 1936, he was pushing Phillips and Rahv, who were disgusted with the "official" literary left, toward a "vague Trotskyism." [16] In September, while the two editors were engaged in discussions and negotiations with the League of American Writers, Farrell argued the view that they should sever all ties.[17] A month later, he noted his dismay at a report that they had made a temporary peace with the Stalinists.[18] At the end of December, Farrell again had hopes that their public break was in the offing, and arranged a meeting for Phillips and Rahv with Socialist party leader Norman Thomas, although it never materialized.[19] During that same phase (spring, summer, and fall 1936) Farrell also chronicled encounters with other dissident intellectuals, such as Edmund Wilson and Harold Rosenberg. These discussions often centered around the Trotsky question.[20]

From the time he joined the Trotskyist movement, George Novack's literary productivity markedly increased. Under the pseudonym "John Marshall," he published two installments in the *New International* late in 1934, touching on various utopian theories. These were followed by a series analyzing the social base and function of intellectuals from a Marxist view, and tracing the evolution of the American intelligentsia during the early years of the Depression. The bulk of Novack's literary output, however, concerned studies of different aspects of American history.[21]

Farrell offered an unmistakable portrait of the young George Novack, serving in his capacity as Secretary of the American Committee for Defense of Leon Trotsky, in the story, "Tom Carroll." Although it was largely composed in the late 1930s, this fiction much resembles Farrell's more explicitly philosophical works which became predominant in the 1950s. Along with the story, "Judith," with which it was published in 1973 (in *Judith and Other Stories*), "Tom Carroll" is also an unusual demonstration of Farrell's abilities at characterization when treating a social milieu qualitatively different from that in his better known works (that is, the Chicago South Side). In these two pieces, "Judith" and "Tom Carroll," Farrell attains a maturity lacking in several previous attempts to write about intellectuals.[22] In "Judith," he integrates strict realism with delicacy of psychological insight to probe the emotional nuances of an affair between two artists whose respective commitments dominate their lives. "Tom Carroll" is also the portrait of an intellectual, but of one whose work appears to have lost its meaning in a mid-1930s maelstrom of political turmoil and his own marital disintegration.

Farrell employs a technique of contrasting characterization so that the figures in "Tom Carroll," an intellectual drama of the 1930s (but with far-reaching philosophical implications), illuminate each other. The superficial vehicle of the story is the typical Farrell theme of lost dreams, especially displayed through Tom Carroll's juxtaposed disillusionment with love (through his relationship to Ruth, his wife) and politics (through his relationship to Bill, his son). Although the internal organization of the story is loose (corresponding to Farrell's narrative mode of thoughts, reminiscences, and dialogues), its overall structure is balanced by the interplay of different themes. It opens on a political note (involving Bill) and closes on a sexual one (with Ruth).

Tom Carroll is a composite figure, suggesting a variety of radicals from the anti-Stalinist intellectual left. A famous historian and biographer of Whitman—whose stature as a scholar and Progressive approaches that of John Dewey and Charles Beard— Carroll had been friends with John Reed, opposed the First World War, hailed the Russian Revolution, and worked to prevent the execution of Sacco and Vanzetti. Now, in his early fifties, he suffers from mysterious stomach pains, sees his twenty-five-year-old son transformed into an arrogant Stalinist, ponders over the absence of love between his wife and himself, and reassesses his political beliefs.

Unlike his son, Bill, and unlike the young Trotskyist, Joseph Benton (the character suggestive of Novack), Carroll now believes that humankind is incapable of mastering history. Carroll has replaced the portrait of Trotsky in his study with one of Lincoln. Once he admired Robespierre, now he labels the Jacobin a fanatic. But the story is by no means a didactic political tract, although some of Carroll's beliefs may be the same as some held by Farrell in recent years:

> The great tragedy of our lifetime, the great tragedy of the 20th century, is to be found in Russia. It is what happens when love turns to hatred and when good turns to evil.[23]

In fact, if anything, there is a certain levelling process in "Tom Carroll" so that the political disease of Stalinism is treated dispassionately on the same plane as other social and biological ills.

The character, Joseph Benton, appears in Part II of "Tom Carroll" (a seventy-eight page story). He has come to request that Carroll lend his name to the movement being organized to defend Leon Trotsky against the slanders of the Moscow Trials. He also asks that Carroll address a forthcoming meeting at the Hippodrome in New York where Trotsky's voice will be broadcast from Mexico to the crowd. Benton's background and thoughts are described as follows:

> Joe Benton had become a Trotskyite because he believed that the life of the world was corrupt, rotten, filthy; and the most rotten, corrupt, and filthy of any group in the world were the intellectuals. But he made an exception of Tom Carroll. He had read Tom's books while he was at Harvard. He had quit Harvard to work in an advertising agency in New York. At that time, he had been a devotee of the philosopher Whitehead, and had objected to Tom's liberalism and pragmatism. But later he had ditched Whitehead for Marx; and now, his opinion of Tom Carroll was that he represented the best liberal tradition in America. But sitting here, talking with him, made him feel sorry for him, superior to him. At the same time there was some fear. He would not want to lock horns with Tom Carroll. Tom knew more than he did about history, but then the man should. But like other liberals, even John Dewey, he did not understand the laws of history.[24]

In an explicit parallel, Tom Carroll compares Benton (Novack) to his own son, the young Stalinist writer, Bill Carroll: Both are zealots who have faith that they can change the course of history. Yet the character of Benton also reveals certain differences. Bill Carroll is blindly arrogant and bigoted; he seeks to manipulate his father into attending a Stalinist meeting to support the Spanish loyalists. Benton, however, is respectful and even has the hope that Trotsky himself can win Carroll to revolutionary Marxist views through discussion. Benton is a young man with noble ideas about truth, philosophy, and the course of history; he seeks to debate and discuss (although cautiously) with Tom Carroll. He does not simply denounce, as does Bill, with slogans and shibboleths. However, it is precisely this idealism of Benton which suggests to Carroll a futility in the Trotskyist movement:

> How did Bill compare with this young fellow? If both of them had their way, they would fight a life-and-death struggle. No, the Trotskyites would probably never be that important.[25]

Tom Carroll's attitude toward Trotsky, despite his rejection of Trotskyist politics, is not completely hostile; he eschews all notions of historical laws, but may see Trotsky (or his cause) as a source for what he believes are more enduring values of truth, integrity, and courage. (In this limited sense, "Tom Carroll" has elements of a dialogue between an older Farrell, transported back to the mid-thirties, and the Stalinists and young Novack of that time.) Carroll's attitude toward Trotsky is similar to the attitude which he also has toward his old lover, Sarah (who appears in the story). But despite his lingering desires for Sarah, as well as a sentimentally motivated agreement to speak in defense of Trotsky, Tom Carroll clearly rejects new liaisons with these two former loves. He judges his past belief in revolution and his old dreams for an enduring sexual love to be romantic illusions, and seeks to adjust to the harsh reality of his middle age.

The character of Tom Carroll may in part reflect Farrell's own views in middle age; but in the 1930s, Farrell's perspective probably would have been more similar (although clearly not identical) to that of the Trotskyist Benton who, in comparing Carroll and Trotsky for the last time before departing, reflects sadly:

> ... he [Carroll] was one of the best of the liberals. And look at him—one of the best. Think of the difference between him and Trotsky.[26]

4.

The Line of Blood

Lines are being drawn between devotion to justice and adherence to a faction, between fair play and a love of darkness that is reactionary in effect no matter what banner it floats.

John Dewey's Speech of May 9, 1937 [1]

The Moscow Trials unfolded at the same time as the Spanish Civil War, the sweep of the Popular Front in France, and the growing fear of fascism against which the Soviet Union seemed a bulwark. In the course of the four trials between 1936 and 1938, Leon Trotsky and other Old Guard Bolsheviks were charged with plotting to assassinate Stalin and other Soviet leaders; conspiring to wreck the Soviet Union's economic and military power; working from the inception of the Revolution for espionage services of Britain, France, Japan, and Germany; and making secret agreements with Hitler and the Mikado to cede vast slices of Soviet territory to imperialist Germany and Japan.[2] The Moscow Trials, as James Farrell marked down in his diary in early 1937, drew a "line of blood" across the decade and the intellectual left.[3]

Farrell began his public attack on the Communist party's politics, from a hybrid of anti-Stalinist and openly Trotskyist positions, in October 1936: In a humorous dialogue in the *Socialist Call*, he satirized the speciously apolitical character of the all-inclusive Popular Front.[4] Two weeks later, Farrell issued a statement explaining why he supported Norman Thomas in the presidential elections. (A similar position was also taken by the Trotskyists who, from early 1936 until late 1937, were an embattled faction in the Socialist party.)

In making this decision, a principal consideration for Farrell was what he believed to be the Socialist party's superior policy toward the threatening war. Farrell pointed out that the Stalinists, because of their new rightward turn, were not calling the impending imperialist war by its real name. Instead, they were fostering an illusion that a war waged by the capitalist United States would simply be "anti-fascist." The Socialist party, Farrell noted in contrast, refused to separate out the question of capitalist causes and socialist solutions from the war issue. He warned that the Communist party was nursing the same sort of delusions that led to the pro-war capitulation of the preponderance of the American intellectual left during World War I. Farrell proudly declined an offer to join the Committee of Professionals for Browder and Ford (the Communist party candidates) because he believed that the purpose of the Stalinist campaign was really to drum up support for Roosevelt, and Farrell predicted that in the face of war Roosevelt's course would merely parallel Wilson's.[5]

By this time Farrell was in the camp of anti-Stalinist radicals and sympathizers of Trotsky, and because of his polemical experience and credentials from the past literary wars, he emerged rapidly as a central organizer. In a letter of October 21, 1936, Farrell noted that he was receiving regular visits from George Novack, and that Novack, who was quite impassioned about political questions, was being "proven right." Farrell also remarked that it was disillusionment over the Moscow Trials which had ultimately pushed him over to supporting Thomas, rather than Browder, in the elections.[6]

The forces gathering for the battle over the Moscow Trials erupted in their first big clash with the appearance of a *New Masses* editorial on November 10: "The *Nation* and Trotsky." A document, published and circulated under the name, "Provisional American Committee for the Defense of Leon Trotsky," had been signed by Norman Thomas, Devere Allen, John Dewey, Horace Kallen, Frieda Kirchway, and Joseph Wood Krutch. The new organization claimed to be neutral and to be concerned primarily about the fact that Trotsky was being held captive by the government of Norway. It was no surprise, the *New Masses* commented, that "Social Democratic traitors" of the Second International like Norman Thomas should be involved. And Krutch, they continued, possessed not only a miserable record in regard to the defense of civil liberties, but had demonstrated prejudice in his capacity on the *Nation* by giving Communist books to Trotskyists to review. John Dewey, the *New Masses* said, was sincere but simply misled.

The *New Masses'* greatest concern, however, was the fact that the document contained a reprint of the October 10 *Nation* editorial, which had asked mildly critical questions about the Moscow Trials. The *New Masses* demanded to know whether the *Nation*'s editorial had been a deliberate preparation for this Trotsky Defense Committee. If the *Nation* was going to support the Trotskyists' "criminal activities," the *New Masses* announced, it should openly declare itself a "Trotskyist mouthpiece" and "organ of a counter-revolutionary band of conspirators and assassins." [7]

The *New Masses'* blast against the *Nation* elicited an immediate response. Frieda Kirchway, the magazine's editor, resigned from the new Committee and the *Nation*'s criticisms of the trials diminished. The record shows that despite occasional waverings and doubts, the *New Republic* and the *Nation* were hardly neutral in their positions throughout the years of the trials. They tacitly if not explicitly sided with the Stalinist regime in a belief that the defendants were guilty of "something," and ultimately they sought to undermine the Dewey Commission of Inquiry and discredit its verdicts. Furthermore, the journals accurately reflected much of the opinion of that section of the liberal intellectual community which, now that the Communist party had turned to the right, desired the maintenance of unity among what they conceived as a progressive bloc of the United States and Soviet Union. Thus, the pro-Stalinist liberals hoped to reduce the disruptive discussion of the trials.[8]

The statement of the Provisional Committee was followed by a press release on behalf of a fullfledged Committee. The additional list of supporters included Farrell, Edmund Wilson, and Max Eastman. This body expanded its province to that of aiding in the formation of an International Commission to examine the information available on the Moscow Trials. Sidney Hook, as a member of the Executive body, was one of those assigned to locate responsible participants.[9]

The December 15, 1936 *New Masses* featured Mike Gold on "Migratory Intellectuals," an article which aimed to undermine the impact of James T. Farrell's open break with Stalinism. Attempting to incite anti-intellectual prejudice, Gold referred to the "Phi Beta Kappa Trotskyites" who were always out to criticize the "low-brow" Stalinists. Gold claimed that in a 1932 discussion with Sidney Hook the aloof professor had announced that the Stalin, Lovestone (Bukharin) and Trotsky factions were all "equally good." Gold also stated that although Hook and other "Trotskyists" had supported the Communist party in the 1932 elections, they then decided that since they knew everything, they should be in charge. Although they soon broke from the party, these alleged "Trotskyist" intellectuals found the doors of the liberal journals "wide open" to them. This was because their hatred of the Communist parties of the world was far greater than their opposition to capitalism, Gold charged. He attributed this "Trotskyist" treachery to vanity, careerism, and indiscipline, and cited Farrell as a recent victim of the disease.

Farrell allegedly lived in the "insular" world of the literary circles of Paris, Chicago, and New York, and was one of the types who aspired to reconcile Communism with a successful career. But, Gold maintained, Communism and the Communist party cannot be separated; the New York Trotskyist intellectuals had proved that they could not be loyal to any party. After comparing Sidney Hook, Anita Brenner, and James T. Farrell unfavorably with Earl Browder, Gold concluded that the current fracas was just one more occurrence of a migration of apostate intellectuals who tended to cluster around the *New Masses* and then leave.[10]

In November 1936, Farrell became active in the Trotsky Defense Committee, and served as a member of its Executive Committee. On November 13, he attended a meeting at George Novack's house which included Novack and Elinor Rice (his first wife, who later wrote biography and fiction), Charles Malamuth (who later translated Trotsky's *Stalin*), Eleanor Clark, Max Nomad, Felix Morrow, Charles Yale Harrison, and Harold and Viola Isaacs.[11]

Soon afterwards, Farrell and Novack attended a cocktail party honoring the publication of *The Best of Art Young*, an anthology of the radical cartoonist. Fifteen years later, Mary McCarthy recorded Farrell's approach to her, which helped launch her on a memorable peregrination among the left intellectuals:

> I was standing, rather bleakly, by the refreshment table, when a question was thrust at me: did I think Trotsky was entitled to a hearing? It was a novelist friend of mine, dimple-faced, shaggy-headed, earnest, with a whole train of people, like a deputation, behind him.[12]

Mary McCarthy acknowledged that Trotsky had the right to asylum and a hearing and soon found herself in the midst of the controversy. In his diary, Farrell recorded that at that same party he had been successful in obtaining five signatures of support: from Clara Gruening Stillman, Burton Rascoe, Lewis Gannett, Ernest Meyer, and Manuel Komroff. He also noted that when Max Lerner refused to sign, he argued with him, and then "let George Novack sic into him." Later, in the heat of the debate, Farrell recalled that he shook his fist in Alexander Trachtenberg's face and dared him to repeat what Farrell believed were slanders.[13]

George Novack was designated the Secretary of the American Committee for Defense of Leon Trotsky. In the recollection of Felix Morrow, the choice was partially a compromise due to some past friction between Trotskyist sympathizers (some from the former *Menorah Journal* group) and Trotskyist party members (especially himself). Morrow recalled that although he gave himself fully to the organized Trotskyist movement from 1933 on, Elliot Cohen (who never joined the party) and Herbert Solow (who was briefly a party member) always kept an "arm's length relationship":

> This led to some coolness, and even antagonism, between us, later, when it came time to merge the Non-Partisan Labor Defense [NPLD] with the [Socialist party's] Workers Defense League. I ran the NPLD, and devoted a great deal of time to

it, but for me it [the work in the NPLD] was simply a party assignment from the Trotskyist party. For Elliot [Cohen] and Herbert [Solow], however, it was their only political base. Hence, when the Trotskyists decided to liquidate the NPLD as part of the necessary steps to get into the Socialist Party, a decision which for me was a simple two plus two arithmetic, Elliot and Herbert were very angry with me and looked upon me as an apparatchik who was mechanically doing the party's bidding. The Trotskyists had to pack the NPLD in order to get a majority vote for the merger with the Workers Defense League. The *Menorah* Group's anger with me for this resulted, a few months later, in their refusing to accept me as the Secretary of the Committee for Defense of Leon Trotsky. They insisted on naming someone else. The Trotskyists compromised with them on a mutually acceptable candidate, who was George Novack. I was named assistant secretary. In actual fact, however, I ran that Committee since that was what the Trotskyist party wanted and this became a full-time job for me during the life of the Committee.[14]

George Novack's recollection adds another perspective:

It may have been as he [Morrow] surmises, that the opposition of Cohen, Solow, et al., was one of the factors in the choice [of the Committee's Secretary] but another may have been because I had superior connections, had already been secretary of the first Trotsky committee in 1934, and was more diplomatic in dealing with non-party people. In any event, it is true that he [Morrow] did as much work and took as much responsibility and deserves as much credit in that endeavor as I. I thought of ourselves as a working team. When I went to Mexico with the [Sub-] Commission or took an extended vacation, he took charge of the office.[15]

In addition to Novack and Morrow, other Trotskyist party members (such as James Burnham and Harold Isaacs) played leading roles in the Committee, along with political sympathizers (Farrell), and allies with distinctly different orientations (Benjamin Stolberg, Sidney Hook, and Suzanne La Follette).[16]

Suzanne La Follette, a relative of of the late Senator Robert La Follette, was an art critic and journalist who had edited the *New Freeman* in the late twenties and early thirties. She was a close friend of Ben Stolberg, who in those years was a leading American writer on labor movements, and a respected critic of books dealing with social and economic problems.

Two striking memoirs of Stolberg—one in Louis Adamic's *My America* (1938) and another in Albert Halper's *Good-bye, Union Square* (1974)—portray Stolberg as a man with a brilliant mind evidenced especially in conversation and journalism. He also possessed erudition animated by a wicked wit.[17] A native of Germany, Stolberg came to the United States at age seventeen and rose from poverty to graduate from Harvard in 1918. After graduate work in sociology at the University of Chicago, and some teaching and editing, Stolberg became a free-lance publicist. He was especially popular in liberal journals and particularly with the *Nation.* According to Adamic, Stolberg had an "intellect cast upon European cultural lines" and had showed sympathy for Trotsky as early as 1931.

At the beginning of 1937, while doing preparatory work for a book on Guatemala, Adamic was suddenly informed that his visa was not to be renewed and he was forced to leave that country. Upon returning to the United States, he learned that Stolberg had announced him an endorser of the American Committee for Defense of Leon Trotsky. Stolberg had done this after having received no objection to a letter he had sent Adamic in Guatemala. Adamic then surmised that the letter must have been confiscated by the Guatemalan authorities because of its letterhead stationery, and that this had been the cause of his visa troubles. Justifiably angered, and also irritated because he felt that the name, the American Committee for "Defense" of Leon Trotsky, sounded too partisan, Adamic wrote a letter of resignation. But, as would also be the case with Mary McCarthy, subsequent pressure from the Stalinists caused Adamic to react. He decided to stick with the Committee and he even became somewhat involved:

> I wrote a letter to the American Committee for the Defense of Leon Trotsky, asking my name to be removed from its roster. Before I mailed it, diverse "Stalinists" and anti-Trotskyites

and professional, neurotically loyal, and well-meaning friends of the Soviet Union pounced on me. Resign! Resign! If I did not resign I might eventually be sorry. It was all right for John Dewey to get mixed up in a thing like this; he was past 70, while I was young. His name was so well established that it could not readily be unfavorably affected in the long run. It was hinted to me that should I ever want to go to the USSR I might be unable to get a visa. My books might never be translated into the Russian.

Adamic found himself attending a few meetings and was eventually glad that he had become involved, although he never felt fully comfortable with the Committee's composition:

The Committee was run by a few deeply interested and intensely motivated persons who were obviously Trotskyites, that is, who believed in Trotsky's conspirational-revolutionary ideas. The idea to clear Trotsky as a matter of principle of justice was probably clear and paramount only in John Dewey's mind; I admired him for it. A few people of the Committee's inner group, as well as most of the Dewey Commission, were more or less pro-Trotsky personally. They admired some part of his mind or past, without agreeing entirely with his basic philosophy and future aims. Politically they were "anti-Stalinist" without being Trotskyite. They were outraged by the trials and executions. I think that Ben Stolberg, Suzanne La Follette, and John Chamberlain were of this group. Otherwise the idea among the Committee leaders was, for the most part, politically pro-Trotsky (i.e., pro-conspiracy, pro-Revolution) in purpose.[18]

Even Farrell, far more involved and supportive of the Committee than Adamic, had his doubts and hesitations about the Trotskyists. When Trotsky arrived in Mexico on January 9, 1937, George Novack and Max Shachtman, along with Frida Kahlo (companion of Diego Rivera), were there to meet him.[19] A few weeks later Farrell recorded a Saturday night meeting of the Trotsky Defense Committee. At the gathering Novack and Shachtman reported on their trip to Mexico, and Farrell noted that "The idolatry of Trotsky on the part of the Trotskyists sometimes gets so thick that it could be cut with a knife." [20]

Nevertheless, Farrell's dedication to the cause remained steadfast. As he wrote to Norman Thomas in late January:

> The consequences of these trials, no matter what the story, are tragic and dreadful, and I fear they must be met.[21]

On January 2, Farrell published a full-page approving review of Max Shachtman's *Behind the Moscow Trials* in the *Socialist Call*. He hailed the book as an important documentation of inconsistencies in the claims of the Moscow inquisition, and he denounced the *New Republic* for its docile acceptance of the guilty verdict that came out of the Moscow Trials.[22] In February, Farrell and John Chamberlain submitted a letter to the *Socialist Call* and *New Republic* explaining why they were supporting the Trotsky Defense Committee, although they were "neither Stalinists nor Trotskyists," and still maintained "friendship for the USSR." [23]

In March 1937, the American Committee for Defense of Leon Trotsky officially established the body which would become popularly known as the "Dewey Commission": The Preliminary Commission of Inquiry into the Charges Made Against Leon Trotsky in the Moscow Trials.[24] Its announced purpose was to gather all the facts about the Moscow Trials proceedings in which Trotsky and his son, Leon Sedov, were the principal accused, and to render a judgment. It was the "subcommission" of this body which conducted the famous thirteen hearings in Coyoacan, Mexico, from April 10 to April 16, 1937. According to Novack:

> During these sessions it [the subcommission]received Trotsky's testimony and that of his secretary, Jan Frankel, cross-examined both witnesses, heard Trotsky's answer to the charges against him, and his counter-charges against the Soviet government. It accepted, subject to verification, such documentary evidence as he had to introduce.[25]

John Dewey was chairman of the Preliminary Commission and the Subcommission; Suzanne La Follette was secretary of the Commission.[26]

In February, although Farrell was preoccupied with the censorship case of Sumner versus *A World I Never Made,* he nevertheless took time to attend a meeting at Novack's house where Angelica Balabanov discussed Spain. He also concerned himself with the Stalinists' efforts to pressure people into quitting the Trotsky Defense Committee—an effort which had resulted in four recent resignations.[27] Toward mid-February Farrell learned from William Phillips that Malcolm Cowley was heading a body whose purpose was to break up the Trotsky Defense Committee. Ferdinand Lundberg, author of *America's Sixty Families* (1937), was also an object of Farrell's concern. Lundberg had been subject to harassment because of his endorsement of the Committee. He had been told that his books were going to suffer, and Farrell frequently had to work on him to strengthen his resistance to pressures to drop off the Committee.[28]

On February 16, a letter signed by fifty writers, editors, and artists appeared in the *New Masses,* warning liberal members of the Trotsky Defense Committee that they were being used. The names included Lillian Wald, Heywood Broun, Colonel Raymond Robins, Max Lerner, Louis Fischer, Newton Arvin, Corliss Lamont, Robert S. Lynd, Theodore Dreiser, Bernard Smith, and Lillian Hellman.[29]

At the same time, Farrell persevered in his reading and study of writings by Trotsky. His approach to the material was not uncritical, however, as is evidenced by his opinions on certain aspects of the philosophical method. After reading *Lessons of October,* Farrell noted in his diary that Trotsky's

> method is concerned with principles, deductions, laws; Trotsky treats tendencies and class positions as if they were possessed of the same momentum as certain tendencies in nature which have been organized in terms of scientific law.[30]

In March 1937, Farrell was present at a dinner for André Malraux. There he managed to get into arguments with Henry Roth (author of *Call It Sleep*), Max Lerner, and Corliss Lamont.[31] Roth had just published a statement in the *New Masses* in which he contended that the purpose of the Dewey Commission was not to have Trotsky defend himself, but to permit Trotsky to libel the

USSR. Trotsky, Roth argued, had a "monstrous ego" and wished to see the Soviet Union destroyed if he was unable to possess it himself.[32]

In the weeks prior to the Mexican hearings, Farrell devoted much time to the activities of the Defense Committee. This increased his interaction with the Trotskyists. Diary notations from this period offer insight into his relations with both the Committee and the organized Trotskyist movement. On March 18, Farrell noted that George Novack had called to inform him of Suzanne La Follette's receiving a letter from Trotsky urging more rapid action in forming the Commission of Inquiry. It was Farrell's understanding that he was supposed to serve on it.[33] On March 22, Farrell recorded a meeting at Suzanne La Follette's house. There Farrell met V. R. Dunne—one of the Trotskyist leaders of the 1934 Minneapolis strikes—whom he described as "genuine, simple, unaffected, tender, a rough-looking little man who has the appearance of an actor. He is unpresuming." James Cannon, however, struck Farrell as vain:

> Cannon seems like a ham actor. He patronized me, and said he was going to straighten me out so I could write better novels, novels with more pity and feeling. . . . I'm not of a mind to be put in his [Cannon's] vest pocket.

Farrell also reported that Suzanne La Follette "is falling heavily for the Trotskyists," and he was disturbed to learn that for some reason he was no longer wanted on the Commission of Inquiry.[34]

The next day, Farrell wrote that he had talked to Philip Rahv, who had seen Cannon at Lionel Abel's house.[35] Rahv claimed that Cannon had been very drunk and boasted about telling John Dewey it was his "moral duty" to be on the Commission of Inquiry. Farrell recorded that he had subsequently complained to George Novack about this incident, and commented that if he were in the Trotskyist party, "I would form an opposition against him [Cannon]." [36] His relations with Cannon, however, grew more friendly over the course of time.

On March 28, Farrell attended a meeting of the Executive Committee of the Trotsky Defense Committee where there were several disputes. The most important one concerned the decision to add Arthur Garfield Hays to the Commission. Farrell and Stolberg feared that Hays was too close to the Stalinists.[37]

Two days later another Executive Committee meeting was held, at Ben Stolberg's. Farrell recorded that he (Farrell) had joined the Executive Committee "in order to protect Trotsky from the Trotskyists," and also to have some say over the decisions, since his name was so frequently connected with the Committe's actions. Farrell noted that at this meeting he was faced with a "fait accompli" from "the boys" (that is, the Trotskyists: Novack, Burnham, and Morrow) in regard to Hays. Apparently, in his opinion, the three had gone ahead on their own in the matter. Farrell wrote:

> All through the meeting I got the feeling more and more that politics is a dragnet and once you get caught in it, you are very likely to be diverted from your career and the work that you can do most competently, and that you are very likely to be ruined.

Farrell added:

> Trotsky is a great man. But that does not mean that one should be a disciple.[38]

It was only several months later, in July, that the reason why Farrell had not been asked to serve on the Commission was clarified. Felix Morrow informed Farrell that although George Novack had wanted Farrell to serve on the Commission, Stolberg had objected strongly and called Farrell "irresponsible." There may have been some friction between Stolberg and Farrell and perhaps between Stolberg and others on the Committee. Nevertheless, Farrell recalled that internal conflicts on the Committee were less of a plague than it might seem from some of his recorded diary annotations; differences came up, but they were eventually settled. Farrell does remember, though, that there was a tendency for Stolberg to want to dominate the Committee.[39]

Farrell's experiences in Mexico have been carefully and thoughtfully described in his two essays commemorating Dewey and

Trotsky.[40] His thoughts during the Commission hearings were recorded in a number of letters written from Mexico. Farrell undertook the trip to Mexico because of personal interest and curiosity; he had no official task. He traveled there in a small group that included Dewey, Stolberg, La Follette, Novack, and Pearl Kluger (secretary of the Subcommission). On the train Dewey engaged in preparatory work and, although he was seventy-eight, seemed to have been interested in everything except his own personal safety. On April 9, the night before the hearings opened, Farrell participated in carrying bricks to be used in the six-foot barricades which protected the windows of the Rivera villa, where the hearings were held. The evidence and arguments presented during the hearings proved Trotsky's innocence conclusively to Farrell. Writing on the day prior to termination of the sessions, Farrell stated to Margaret Marshall of the *Nation:*

> It is a shame that you are not here to attend the hearings. It is a spectacle to see, a spectacle rare in history. Imagine Robespierre or Cromwell under such circumstances. Well this is more, because neither Cromwell nor Robespierre had the intellectual breadth that Trotsky has. And it should go down on the record that the editorial policy of the *Nation* on this question is a scandal, which makes one hope that the *Nation* will be eternally disgraced for its double dealing and cowardice on this issue. . . .

> Trotsky has utterly demolished the macabre fables of the Moscow Trials for any human being who is susceptible to reason and who does not require that his opinions be manufactured for him by persons thousands of miles across the sea. . . . He has built up a logical case, and despite the fact that he has gone on answering questions almost six hours a day since Saturday, his testimony holds together like a most amazing piece of logic. This is a spectacle I have never expected to witness in my life.[41]

During the hearings Farrell held a number of conversations with Trotsky. In one of these he mentioned that Trotsky had appeared to some American radicals as "romantic," an idea that Trotsky did not like. In another discussion, Trotsky seemed to be pressing Farrell to make some kind of political commitment to the Fourth International (founded by Trotsky and his followers in 1938, but in preparation from 1933 onward). Farrell, however, indicated that his primary concern upon return to the United States would be the writing of novels. Trotsky and Farrell also discussed literature:

> He [Trotsky] asked questions about American literature and spoke of having read *Babbitt,* but his admiration for Lewis was qualified. The character of Babbitt seemed unintelligent to him. I spoke of Dreiser whom I praised as a great writer but whose philosophical and general ideas I thought sometimes banal. Trotsky asked how could a man be a great writer if his ideas were stupid. "What American writers need," he said, "is a new perspective." [42]

The reaction of the Stalinist press to the Mexican hearings was one of outrage. The editorial of the April 20 *New Masses* was titled "Trotsky Investigates Himself." It described "Dewey's Little Band" as follows: Goldman was a Trotskyist; Stolberg was a "fake"; La Follette was "under Stolberg's influence"; Rühle was allegedly an "active Trotskyist"; Beals was supposedly "hostile to the USSR." Tresca, the former IWW leader and anarchist, was the only one whom the *New Masses* acknowledged to have a legitimate connection with the labor movement. Charles Rumford Walker, who handled publicity for the Subcommission, was in the *New Masses'* view a "Trotskyist propagandist allied with the Dunne Brothers." And Dewey was not impartial either: The *New Masses* charged that he had been influenced by his former students, Eastman and Hook. So Trotsky, the *New Masses* concluded, was merely being investigated by his own followers.[43]

Responding to a letter from Kenneth Patchen, which the poet sent from Hollywood, Farrell vented his anger against the Stalinist fellow travelers:

> I do not think that we can analyze the intellectual conduct of our contemporaries who live by faith alone, as a purely

individual phenomenon. It is a social manifestation, and they, in living by faith in the Comintern alone, become part of a system. It impresses me more and more as a system which prevents a person from owning his own mind, his own convictions, his own feelings. And it is, in consequence, utterly inimical to writers.[44]

After returning to the United States, Farrell opened up an attack once more against the Stalinist literary movement. This time he presented documentation of the Communist literary orientation's failure to produce substantial fiction in an article called, "The Last Writers' Congress: An Interim Report on Its Results." [45] Farrell also participated in a heated exchange of letters concerning Frederick Schuman's assessment of Trotsky in the *Southern Review*. Among other things, Farrell charged that Schuman had ignored the importance of the Comintern debate on the Chinese Revolution of 1926 and 1927, and he had purposefully misquoted the title of a Trotsky piece on terrorism.[46]

That same summer, while continuing to battle censors' attempts to ban his novels from sale, Farrell also resumed his polemics in the *Socialist Call*. His weekly column was called "The Cultural Front." On July 17 Farrell lashed out against the *Nation*'s claim to neutrality regarding the Moscow Trials. On the 24th he addressed a satirical letter to the Second American Writers' Congress. On August 21, he discussed the *Nation* again, this time challenging the editors with printing false statements about the murder of Andrés Nin, leader of the Spanish POUM. On August 28, Farrell favorably reviewed Trotsky's *The Stalin School of Falsification.*[47]

In addition, Farrell maintained his connections with the major literary-political dissident current, which had yet to break publicly with the Stalinist movement. This grouping had originated with *Partisan Review* (temporarily discontinued during most of 1937), and surfaced as an oppositional bloc at the Second American Writers' Congress with a few additional individuals. Phillips, Rahv, and their new allies then relaunched the journal, *Partisan Review*, near the end of 1937.

In late May 1937, Farrell reported in his diary word of a meeting held to discuss a possible anti-Stalinist intervention into the

American Writers' Congress. He had heard that those present included Philip Rahv, William Phillips, Mary McCarthy, James Rorty, Eleanor Clark, Margaret Marshall, Bruno Fischer, and Herbert Solow.[48] Although a memorable intervention was staged there by Rahv, Macdonald, McCarthy, Phillips, and Clark in the Critics Workshop, and another by Trotskyist Harry Roskolenko (following a talk by Albert Rhys Williams),[49] Farrell did not attend the Congress. In his diary, Farrell recorded that he did not participate because tickets were sold out when he inquired, and he was against asking any special favors of the Stalinists.[50] Also, Farrell saw little point in trying to disrupt the conference, especially since he did not have a strong impression of the abilities of some of those who planned to intervene.[51]

During the summer of 1937, Farrell followed the fortunes of the Trotskyist movement, becoming quite disturbed by the factional struggle in which the Trotskyists were embroiled inside the Socialist party. Farrell heard one version of the dispute from Gus Tyler (a leading Socialist), who claimed that the Trotskyist faction was about to split from the Socialist party; then he heard another story from Felix Morrow, who insisted that the Trotskyists were being expelled. Farrell concluded that he himself should avoid getting involved in the fracas, especially for fear that his work might be disrupted.[52] But still he kept in touch; for example, on August 23, Farrell recorded that a number of delegates from the Young Peoples Socialist League had arrived from Chicago for a convention, and that among them was "a young Trotskyist named Saul Bellow who is also an editor of *Beacon* magazine."[53]

Although Farrell was not directly involved in the reorganization of *Partisan Review* on an anti-Stalinist basis, he was a concerned supporter of the venture. For some time before, and especially back in December 1936 and January 1937, Farrell had urged Phillips and Rahv to break with the Communists openly, and he had attempted to enlist the support of Norman Thomas for them, arranging a meeting which they apparently declined to attend.[54] In answer to an inquiry, George Novack wrote:

> . . . it is not true that he [Phillips] and Rahv became anti-Stalinist simultaneously with Farrell. I remember very well

that for almost two years after Farrell became indoctrinated with our [Trotskyist] ideas and was pulling away from the Communist party, one of his [Farrell's] preoccupations was the unwillingness and hesitancy of Rahv and Phillips to do so. The scuttling of the John Reed Clubs and the Moscow Trials decided that for them.[55]

(However, in an interview William Phillips stated that he did not recall Farrell becoming anti-Stalinist prior to the rest of the *Partisan Review* group: "I believe I turned against them just as early, but people remember things differently." [56])

In December 1937, Farrell's name headlined the red cover of the first issue of the new *Partisan Review* along with Edmund Wilson, Pablo Picasso, Sidney Hook, and Dwight Macdonald. Farrell's contribution was an excerpt from his forthcoming novel *No Star is Lost*. Additionally, in his *Socialist Call* column, Farrell attacked the *New Masses'* claim that Phillips and Rahv had "stolen" *Partisan Review* from its rightful owners. Farrell emphasized that he spoke with authority on the matter, inasmuch as he had contributed far more to the original publication than the currently irate Communist party members who had once had their names listed on *Partisan Review*'s masthead. Farrell pointed out that after the John Reed Clubs had disbanded, it was Phillips and Rahv, along with Alan Calmer, who had kept the journal alive; and furthermore, Farrell charged that Granville Hicks had favored its liquidation back in 1935.[57]

Farrell rounded out the year 1937 on the literary-political front with a review of a collection of papers from the Second American Writers' Congress. In a hard-hitting critique from the left, Farrell demonstrated how in several areas—such as the Congress's stand on war and Joseph Freeman's startling political reassessment of Mexican president Cardenas—the Congress proceedings had manifested the Popular Front transmogrification.[58]

The *New Masses,* in turn, maintained its polemics against Farrell and the Dewey Commission supporters through 1937 and into 1938. Their assaults ranged from crude satirical poems [59] to more rational attempts to discredit their work. For example, Stanley Randolph employed mild satire in "Mr. Dewey Stakes His

Reputation" (describing a December 12, 1937 public meeting of the Trotsky Defense Committee in New York). Randolph asserted that George Novack, "a member of the Trotskyite center," had opened the event with insistent and suspicious-sounding pleas that the Committee was interested only in facts and truth and not politics and that arguments had been made that Stolberg, Chamberlain, and Tresca were not partisan. After mocking these claims, the author went on to insist that the Chairman, Dewey, was simply not competent to judge the trials.[60]

Robert Forsythe (pseudonym for drama critic Kyle Crichton), wrote "Is John Dewey Honest?" and commented on a radio address by the aged philosopher on the Trials. Dewey was not a Trotskyist and not a fascist, Forsythe magnanimously conceded, "just a world-famous philospher allowing himself to be used by the Trotskyites and fascists." [61] The January 18 editorial of the *New Masses* was titled, "Stolberg Stool-Pigeon"; it labeled the journalist a Trotskyist and declared Stolberg an ally of reaction because he had blamed the Communist party for some of the CIO's problems (in an article published by Scripps-Howard papers).[62] The February 1 *New Masses* hailed the *Nation*'s denunciation of left-wing criticisms which had been made of the Comintern's policy of "Collective Security." Farrell, one of the critics, was described as an "open Trotskyite" and Lewis Corey as a "slightly concealed Lovestoneite," but they were said to be identical in aiding the fascists (through their opposition to Comintern policy).[63] On February 1, Robert Forsythe wrote "The Disintegration of Mr. Stolberg," calling him a "well-known parlor fink." Forsythe contended that a "miasmal haze" hung over anyone who ever got close to Trotsky.[64] Two weeks later, an additional *New Masses'* recrimination was contributed by Bruce Minton. "Checkup on Stolberg" charged that over a decade of collusion had occurred between Stolberg and the Trotskyists, and that a pernicious method of "falsification and distortion" was employed in Stolberg's articles on the CIO.[65]

Farrell's political association with the Trotskyist party remained restrained throughout the remainder of the 1930s. He traveled in Europe for four months, and published *No Star is Lost* (1938), *Tommy Gallagher's Crusade* (1939), and *Father and Son* (1940). After the Moscow Trials, Farrell was in close touch with only one or two of the Trotskyists (for example, George Novack). When Max Shachtman and James Burnham published their provocative article, "Intellectuals in Retreat," in the January 1939 *New International,* Farrell was surprised to find his own name thrown in with a roster of intellectuals abandoning revolutionary Marxism. Farrell conjectured that Shachtman and Burnham tossed him into their article because they imagined he was thinking along those lines, although there was no evidence for it. (Surprised when he read the article, Farrell asked them why they had included his name; they had no answer.) [66] In addition, Farrell was offended by the character of the polemic and remarked of the Trotskyist authors in his diary:

> They've shut the door in everyone's face and were tactless, stupid and silly, using gossip and falsifications.[67]

Farrell also participated in the formation and some activities of the League for Cultural Freedom and Socialism, which allied *Partisan Review* writers with Trotskyist writers such as James Burnham, Sherry Mangan, George Novack, Harry Roskolenko, and John Wheelwright.[68] In addition, Farrell was present as an observer during a Trotskyist-initiated demonstration against a Nazi gathering at Madison Square Garden.[69] Afterwards, Farrell wrote an open letter of protest to Mayor LaGuardia, demanding to know why the police had attacked the demonstration and protected the Nazis. Farrell emphasized that such a policy of giving "police protection to fascists and clubs to anti-fascists" was reminiscent of events in Italy and Germany.[70] In a lighter vein, Farrell also organized a baseball team, the "Studs Lonigan A.C.," composed of people from the anti-Stalinist milieu, including Max Eastman, Sidney Hook, John McDonald, Dr. David Glusker (husband of Anita Brenner), and Arthur Pincus.[71]

In the fall of 1939, Farrell followed the new dispute erupting inside the Trotskyist party. This concerned primarily theoretical and practical problems of the social character of the Soviet State and ruling regime, but also organizational and philosophical matters. Factional lines were being drawn, especially over whether the Soviet Union still remained what Trotsky had designated a "workers' state" with "bureaucratic deformations," or whether it might be some new form of class society. In early October, Farrell expressed doubts about the workers' state thesis in his diary, in light of the Soviet invasion of Poland.[72] A few weeks later, however, he commented favorably on Trotsky's contribution to the discussion, "The USSR in War," which appeared in the *New International:* he called it a "brilliant article." (Farrell also noted Trotsky's statement that if the Western proletariat failed to consummate a revolution after the next war, the fundamentals of Marxism would have to be re-evaluated.) [73]

In the following weeks, Farrell worried over the dispute. He noted that Felix Morrow had declared for Cannon's side in opposition to Shachtman and Burnham, and he criticized what he saw as hypocritical elements in Albert Goldman's position.[74] Farrell's December entries tend to indicate a growing sympathy for the view of Shachtman and Burnham. On December 1, he stated opposition (in his diary) to the analysis of the *Socialist Appeal* newspaper on the Soviet-Finnish War (which reflected the view of Cannon's and Trotsky's faction) and on December 10 Farrell recorded his dislike of Trotsky's article, "A Petty-Bourgeois Opposition." Also, in his diary, Farrell wrote out a refutation of Trotsky's philosophical views expressed in that article's section on "The ABC of Materialist Dialectics." [75]

Farrell had doubts throughout the later thirties about the social nature of the Soviet state during its Stalinist phase, but he was uncertain about exactly how the class nature of the Soviet Union should have been defined. During the fight between the Cannon and Shachtman factions, which resulted in a nearly even split in the membership in the spring of 1940, each of the two factions assigned a person to come around and work on the novelist. Albert Gates (pseudonym for Albert Glotzer) saw Farrell more frequently on behalf of the Shachtman group, and Farrell tended to side mainly with them, although he hesitated to fully accept their theoretical explanation. Farrell also had heterodox views on the methodological questions:

> As far as the philosophical disputes went [Farrell reminisced], I never accepted dialectical materialism as a statement of scientific method. I never accepted Marxism as an authentic

philosophy, although I may have been wrong in that. Years later I read the essays from the famous dispute between Max Eastman and Sidney Hook. I felt that Eastman was a crude empiricist and didn't have as much technique as Hook. Hook's article in the *Marxist Quarterly* was very good. Engels, much more than Marx, formulated dialectics. I never liked Lenin's *Materialism and Empirio-Criticism*. It suffers from the deficiency of the correspondence theory of knowledge. I didn't start approaching the question of dialectical materialism directly through Marx. I had read a lot of philosophy before and thought these aspects of Marxism just didn't make sense.[76]

Farrell's novelette, *Tommy Gallagher's Crusade*, partially stemmed from his involvement with Trotskyism—and especially his support of their anti-fascist campaign of the late thirties. *Tommy Gallagher's Crusade* is the story of a young Irishman who supports a fascist organization led by Father Moylan (a figure suggestive of Father Coughlin). Tommy is unable to maintain a steady job, so he is classified as a lumpenproletarian (which the Trotskyists saw as part of the social base of fascist movements). The following passage depicts a scene where Gallagher and his friends prepare physically to disrupt a Trotskyist street meeting:

> Before they had come, there had been some bitter heckling of the meeting coming from a group of Communists. The speaker had countered the hecklers, and finally they [the Stalinists] had marched off in a dudgeon after calling on all workers assembled to shun this Trotskyite meeting like a plague. . . . When Tommy arrived, he gazed about with an apprehensive look, because there was a bigger crowd than he had counted on. The first words he heard were:

> "When the fascists rear their heads here, only the revolutionary working class can smash them and liberate all mankind from fascism and capitalism. Comrades, fellow workers, friends, this is the lesson of revolutionary defeats suffered in Europe, and this is the lesson we must learn in America before it is too late."

Tommy grinned. The usual boushwah of the Reds, he reflected. . . .

"That is why we have issued calls for a Workers Defense Guard to be prepared to smash the fascist gangs when they raise their heads in America as they have begun to do," the speaker went on.[77]

This passage is essentially a fictionalized version of the Trotskyist program for struggling against fascism. Included is the critique of the Communist party's sectarian refusal to join with other left-wing forces against the fascist movement: the Stalinists denounce and try to break up the very street meeting which the fascists are threatening. Also included is the Trotskyists' call for a united front of all workers and working-class organizations, and the use of mass actions (which visibly intimidate the fascists, in the novelette). Trotsky had argued that the rise of Hitler in Germany was made possible by the Communist party policy which, instead of calling for an alliance with the Social Democrats of Germany, attacked them as "Social fascists" more dangerous than the Nazis. The efficacy of the Trotskyist position is demonstrated on the following page when Gallagher and his gang are repulsed by defense guards. Despite praise given to *Tommy Gallagher's Crusade* at the time of its publication, [78] it must be acknowledged that as a work of imaginative literature it has several characteristic weaknesses of the short "thesis" story: Its tone is too didactic and the characters insufficiently complex.

Farrell's critical writings in 1938 and 1939 included an approving article on Richard Wright's *Uncle Tom's Children*, [79] and an unsigned review of *Not Guilty: Report of the Commission of Inquiry into the Charges Made Against Leon Trotsky in the Moscow Trials*.[80] In a commentary on the works of Ignazio Silone in *Southern Review*, Farrell praised the Italian writer's scientific appraisal of the causes of fascism, but he criticized the conclusion of Spina (in *Bread and Wine*) that the creation of a "moral elite" was the requisite means of opposition. Farrell also observed that while Silone's *Fontamara* had been written from the viewpoint of revolutionary hope and passion, *Bread and Wine* had been produced in a mood of defeat. Farrell concluded by labeling Silone the "foremost postwar novelist of Europe," and explained his own view that, inasmuch as bourgeois democracy had been proven incapable of stopping fascism, the choice of the future lay between "socialism or barbarism." [81]

In a *Partisan Review* symposium, "The Situation in American Writing: Seven Questions," Farrell identified his literary project with the tradition of "modern realism and naturalism." He cited specifically Dreiser, Lewis, Anderson, Hemingway, Lardner, Masters, Sandburg, Proust, and Joyce as his most noteworthy literary inspirers. When asked for his assessment of the contribution of Henry James, Farrell pointed to James' sophisticated conception of time, psychological relativism, and "healthy disciplinary influence." Farrell also averred that he opposed the conception of writing for a specific audience, and that the object of his literary art was to tell the truth. Returning to the problems of the present decade, Farrell argued that a healthy realistic literary tendency had emerged early in the thirties but now, he warned, the gravitation of writers toward the liberal-Stalinist Popular Front was multiplying the danger of cultural nationalism (as a response to war hysteria). Farrell propounded the necessity of maintaining a "critical spirit." [82]

In late August, Farrell justified his opposition to the Second American Writers' Congress in response to a savage recrimination from the journalist Heywood Broun; [83] Farrell also defended John Dos Passos's anti-Stalinist *Adventures of a Young Man.* In this latter article, Farrell argued that, although some critics, like F. W. Dupee and John Chamberlain, favored the novel, others had treated it shallowly or reduced it to politics. Farrell identified Dos Passos with Silone, maintaining that both were writers in search of integrity. He also asserted that a critique of Stalinism (such as was embodied in *Adventures of a Young Man)* was hardly the irrelevant or sectarian issue some critics claimed, inasmuch as it probed the "deadend of a historic movement." True, Farrell conceded, the novel suffered from several of Dos Passos's inveterate weaknesses: The characters seemed typed, perceptions were catalogued, the vernacular was often used without differentiating characters' speeches. But much of the opposition to Dos Passos's book had a political basis, for it antagonized the alliance of the liberal-Stalinist Popular Front.[84]

Among a number of letters of protest and manifestos signed by Farrell, several were particularly noteworthy. On September 21, after the announcement of the Hitler-Stalin Pact, he addressed a letter to the *Nation*. He charged that since the journal had endorsed the Stalinists' policy of Collective Security, opposed the investigators of the Moscow Trials, ignored the anti-Stalinists' criticisms of the conduct of the Comintern in Spain, it was not sufficient for the *Nation* now to merely remove itself "from the Stalinist orbit" by showing indignation at the Hitler-Stalin Pact. Farrell requested that a discussion be reopened on these past issues.[85]

In November, Farrell addressed an open letter to Thomas Mann, who had endorsed the Second American Writers' Congress and accepted an honorary office. Farrell pointed out that this body, which had excluded prominent anti-Stalinist left writers (who were attacked by some of the League of American Writers' members as "agents of fascism"), had not yet responded to the Hitler-Stalin Pact. Since Mann had endorsed the policies of the group prior to the Pact, as well as in his book *The Coming Victory of Democracy*, Farrell asked for Mann's current views.[86]

Farrell ended the decade with an assessment of the left-wing literary record, as incisive as it was provocative. Although it was aimed primarily at political and literary achievements, he carefully warned that the radicals' endeavor did not exhaust all literary aspects of the decade. He noted that William Faulkner, for instance, had produced distinguished work without being directly involved in politics.

The mood of the decade had evolved, according to Farrell, from revolutionary hope at the beginning to despair and fear of imminent fascism at the end. Integral to understanding this transition was the transformation in character and role of the Soviet Union, as its "ruling regime" degenerated into an "obviously counter-revolutionary force." In the early stage the radical writers assumed an arrogance in politics matched only by their ignorance of facts and theory, and they "accepted ready-made political slogans and programs from the Stalinist movement." Farrell offered several careers as paradigmatic responses to the situation. Edmund Wilson was a positive exemplar:

In the early thirties, he joined the spiritual and intellectual migration of writers to the left. However, he retained his judgment, perception, and independence. When new questions were posed, he investigated them in all seriousness. He did not accept ready-made slogans simply because a radical brand was put on them. The result can be seen in his work. Whatever one thinks of the various of his conclusions, Wilson's literary criticism has been the finest written in the last decade. It has revealed a mind that is constantly growing, and constantly enlarging its interests. A similar example, in the case of a younger critic, is Philip Rahv.

Malcolm Cowley, however, exhibited the opposite development:

His criticism during the last decade lacks character, analytical capacity, and breadth of judgment; it is wishy-washy, replete with personal asides, and often it is no more than an oblique application of the "party line" of the moment.

Granville Hicks' work was even more meretricious:

When the party line changed to that of the Popular Front policy in 1935, the character of Mr. Hicks' judgments began to change. He started to praise writers whom he had attacked brutally only shortly before. In the new period as in the old, he continued to lay down the line.

Farrell discoursed on the first years of the Depression decade, and the battle against the Communist movement's literary authoritarianism which, he professed, destroyed the positive aspects of the developing realist movement. Returning to the basis of his revolutionary convictions, Farrell emphasized:

The value of revolutionary movements to culture is that they create a ferment of ideas and forge new perspectives which influence the cultural productions of the future. Such was the contribution of the French Revolution; such was the effect of the Irish national revolution; such for a few years was the effect of the Russian Revolution before the GPU put a uniform on the artist.

With the advent of the Popular Front, a new cultural policy had emerged which

> hastily enlisted commercial writers, high-priced Hollywood scenarists, a motley assortment of mystery plot mechanics, humorists, newspaper columnists, strip teasers, band leaders, glamour girls, actors, press agents, Broadway producers, aging wives with thwarted literary ambitions, and other such ornaments of American culture.

Everyone was welcome, Farrell noted, except anti-Stalinist radicals, who became the object of a ferocious witch hunt. In retrospect, Farrell commented with sobriety, the decade of the 1920s produced more important works in American fiction than had the 1930s. Only a few important novels had emerged—such as Roth's *Call It Sleep,* Algren's *Somebody in Boots,* Dahlberg's *Bottom Dogs,* and some books of Daniel Fuchs, Erskine Caldwell, and John Fante.[87]

Yet Farrell had no intention of disparaging the significance of the 1930s to politics and literature *en bloc;* he sought an assessment within the perspective of the realist-naturalist tradition in which he believed:

> The dominant tradition of twentieth century American literature is one of realism and naturalism. It has produced a literature which has told us, in concrete terms, the cost of American civilization. It has unfolded the patterns of American destiny, posed in terms of individual lives the problems and contradictions of our society, and corrected many latter-day myths. Also, it has also cried out in social protest, and it has set the basis for the creation of the speech of Americans into a language of literature as well as one of life. Most of the newer writers of the 1930s, whether their works be good, bad, or indifferent, have worked in that tradition.

The literary contribution of the 1930s must be acknowledged in its introduction of new types of characters, Farrell noted, "from the bottom and near bottom of American society." Unfortunately, many of the radical writers had been satisfied simply with the novelty of their material, and

> In consequence, there has often been no drive, no struggle revealed to attain a way of seeing life, and an orientation which would permit many of these younger writers to continue growing and expanding, to go back into their material and see in it fresh emphases and additional meanings.

Because of this self-imposed limitation and the dogmatism of the Communist cultural movement, "many of the writers of the 1930s have not fulfilled the promise that was claimed for them."

And what of the 1940s? Farrell's prognosis was bleak:

> Prediction is useless. The generation of writers of the next decade will have to come forth at a time of profound social crisis. The air is full of propaganda, passion, and partisanship. Conditions for writing seem worse daily. The fangs of suppression hang over the writer. The interest of men is getting far from the paths and ways of literature. The coming writer stands amidst a kind of ruin. He must kindle excitement and enthusiasm for his work, confidence in himself, and he must forge his own perspectives. There are no literary movements now. There is little criticism written that is worth the paper on which it is printed. There is more talk of defending culture with bayonets now than of producing culture, and gaining from it those humanizing lessons and values which go so far as to make man civilized. Thus dawn the 1940s. . . . [88]

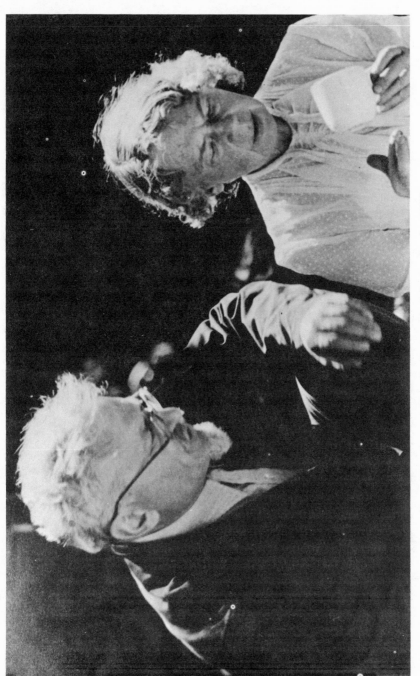

Leon Trotsky and Natalia Sedova in Mexico in the 1930s.

John McDonald, James T. Farrell and Albert Glotzer at the Dewey Commission hearings in Coyoacan, Mexico, in April 1937.

Herbert Solow, Leon Trotsky and Albert Goldman at the Dewey Commission hearings in Coyoacan, Mexico, in April 1937.

Carleton Beals, John Dewey (standing), Suzanne La Follette and Otto Ruhle during the Dewey Commission hearings in Coyoacan, Mexico, in April 1937.

Suzanne La Follette, Benjamin Stolberg, Otto Ruhle and John Dewey during the Dewey Commission hearings in Coyoacan, Mexico, in April 1937.

Jan Frankel, James T. Farrell, Albert Glotzer, Bernard Wolfe and Dorothy Eisner at the home of Frida Kahlo and Diego Rivera in Mexico in April 1937.

James P. Cannon, Martin Abern and Max Shachtman outside the Socialist Workers party offices at 116 University Place in New York City in 1938.

James T. Farrell speaking at the Farewell Banquet for the Minneapolis Eighteen on December 26, 1943. At left: Farrell Dobbs. At right: Alfred Russell, Ted Grant and Karl Kuehn.

James P. Cannon, Felix Morrow and Albert Goldman in the Minneapolis headquarters of the Socialist Workers party before surrendering to U.S. marshals on December 31, 1943.

George Novack, secretary of the Civil Rights Defense Committee, in Washington D.C. on April 2, 1944, to present petitions and resolutions to Presidential Pardon Authority, demanding pardon of the Minneapolis labor case prisoners.

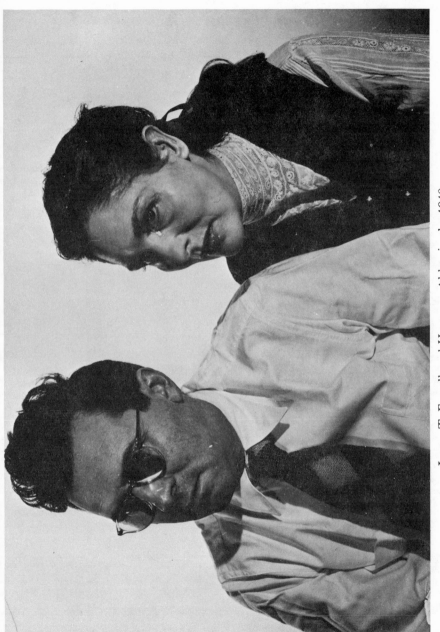

James T. Farrell and Hortense Alden in the 1940s.

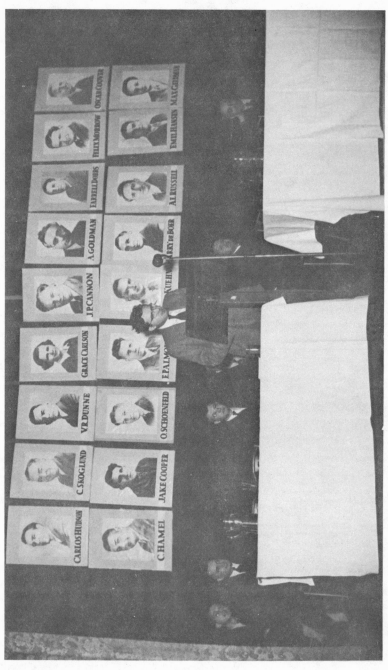

James T. Farrell addressing Welcome Home meeting for the Minneapolis labor case prisoners at the Hotel Diplomat in New York City on February 2, 1945. Left to right: Oscar Schoenfeld, Karl Kuehn, George Novack, Farrell Dobbs (behind speaker), James T. Farrell (at podium), Felix Morrow, Albert Goldman.

5.

Standing Fast

Trotsky represented the last traces of an independent left; I think many radicals are glad he is gone; as you say, he was their forgotten conscience and never spoke without troubling them profoundly. I regret that I am not a poet or a dramatist; I can imagine nothing more stirring than a poem or play about him. He is the real descendant of the great literary romantic heroes of the late 18th and early 19th century, returning from the world of dreams and hopes to the struggle of actual life. He had a vision, acute sense of reality, courage and an absolute integrity. Is there another man in the whole world like that today? The attacks on him from the retreating and vanishing left betray their faithlessness and political insipidity; they offer no action comparable to his own; they are firstly irresponsible. Who dares to take his place? But his life and writings are like a gospel which will awaken new leaders, I am sure.

Meyer Schapiro to Farrell, August 1940 [1]

1940 was the year of Leon Trotsky's assassination by a Stalinist agent in Mexico.[2] That event constituted a momentous assault on

the morale of the anti-Stalinist left.[3] It occurred less than a year
after the Hitler-Stalin Pact and Soviet invasion of Poland in late
1939. Then, many Stalinist fellow travelers and a number of
Communist party intellectuals had fled their movement. And even
some long-term anti-Stalinist radicals were so shaken up that they
renounced their support to the Marxist movement altogether (see,
for example, Max Eastman's *Stalin's Russia and the Crisis in
Socialism*). In the wake of the Pact, the Trotskyist party itself was
thrust into a process of factional strife, and in April 1940 a major
split was consummated. The Socialist Workers party, led by
Cannon, remained true to Trotsky's positions while the Workers
party, headed by Shachtman, was formed as a rival.[4]

Farrell switched his regular column, "The Cultural Front,"
originally in the *Socialist Call,* to *Partisan Review* in 1940. It lasted
about a year. The first installment was a scathing critique of the
fellow travelers of Stalinism. Replying to a letter sent by John
Chamberlain to the *New Republic,* in which Chamberlain proposed
an alliance of older anti-Stalinists and the new ex-Stalinists, Farrell
warned that these ex-travelers had not evidenced any genuine
understanding of the basis of their past errors, and that this was a
prerequisite to serious unity. Farrell's article also articulated a
Third Camp position (renouncing equally the USSR and capitalist
countries) similar to that of the Shachtman group's outlook:

> I have long been an opponent of Stalinism. But I am not in
> favor of an alliance of intellectuals which is based solely on
> opposition to Russia. Such an alliance will only play into the
> hands of our own war mongers. I consider Stalin to be in the
> Hitler war camp and his policies to be Red Imperialism. But
> in order to fight one imperialism, I do not want to join
> another one. I am against both imperialisms.[5]

Ironically, one of Farrell's disagreements with Chamberlain was
precisely over the question of the source, staying power, and real
nature of Stalinism. Since Chamberlain had seen Stalinist ideas
discredited among numerous intellectuals, he now labeled the
movement as dead. Farrell pointed out that such intellectuals had
never been the source of Stalinism, but had simply been used by it:

. . . Stalin never really depended on these men. In fact, he has shot much better men than Louis Fischer, Vincent Sheean, Malcolm Cowley, Granville Hicks, Ralph Bates, and Dr. Frederick L. Schuman.

On the contrary, Farrell maintained, Stalinism had to be understood as a powerful social movement with a material base still in existence. To reckon with it, one required far more reliable allies than the blind ex-Stalinists who had needed a "historic earthquake" to awaken them to realities. "Stalinism is not broken," Farrell affirmed; and almost as a cruel confirmation there occurred the murder of Leon Trotsky in Mexico on August 21, 1940.

On that day, Farrell was in a New York hospital recuperating from a carbuncle operation. When the evening news came over the radio, Farrell became so upset that he had to be given medication to sleep. "I feel terrible about the criminal murder of Leon Trotsky," he wrote his sister, Mary, on the 26th:

> It is a great and tragic loss, especially at this period. We needed Trotsky. The murder, in passing, documents the fact that all these years, I have not been exaggerating when I have tried to tell people what Stalinism is. The murder proves what it is—criminal political gangsterism as vile as fascism itself. But what a miserable and gloomy consolation it is that the assassination of Trotsky proves that we are right in trying to warn people about Stalinism. The crime is unspeakable. There are no words to describe it. I feel stunned, hurt, bitter, impotently in a rage. He was the greatest living man, and they murdered him, and the government of the United States is even afraid of his ashes. God! [6]

Farrell's published tributes to Trotsky at the time, in the press of the Cannon and Shachtman groups and in *Partisan Review*, explain those aspects of Trotsky's life and thought which had been the most meaningful to Farrell.[7] Although he explained that he was not a follower of Trotsky "in the strict and literal meaning of this term," Farrell acknowledged the substantial intellectual influence Trotsky had exerted on him:

Were it not for his writings, I would be a different person than I am, and I would think differently than I do. The loss of Leon Trotsky at this particular moment is tragic. In this black and bitter period of reaction, Trotsky was needed, and needed not merely as a symbol, but even more so as a leader. Now, those points on which one disagreed with him fade in importance. One sees now his greatness, the inspiration which was gained from his very life, from his indomitable fight, and from his brilliant writings. Leon Trotsky was a great revolutionist, a great writer, a great man, a great spirit. Edmund Wilson, the literary critic, once remarked that since his exile from Soviet Russia, Leon Trotsky had served as "the Marxist conscience of the world." With grief, I say farewell to the Old Man. He is dead in the flesh. The spirit that animated his work will not die.

The more elaborate consideration in *Partisan Review* emphasized Trotsky's qualities of personal strength and fortitude; these were the very qualities which Farrell himself had employed in his struggle to break free of the chains of ignorance and religion in the 1920s, and against the Stalinists and Stalinist-liberal alliance in the early and later thirties. Now he was mustering them to fight the creeping war hysteria:

The life of Leon Trotsky is one of the great tragic dramas of modern history. Pitting his brain and will against the despotic rulers of a great empire, fully conscious of the power, the resources, the cunning and cruelty of his enemy, Trotsky had one great weapon at his command—his ideas. His courage never faltered; his will never broke. His children were murdered or driven to suicide; his friends, his co-workers and secretaries were killed. His entire generation was annihilated. He lived the life of a prisoner, continually exposed to the blow of an assassin. He was fatalistic enough to know that he would probably not live to see his ideas triumph. Nevertheless, he accepted without a moment's hesitation all the risks involved in the propagation of his doctrines. Finally, unable to refute his ideas, they drove a pickaxe into his brain.

Farrell praised Trotsky's courage in exile, and underscored the fact that Trotsky had not sought favors from public opinion or state powers, because he was

> big enough to stand alone, always rising to the level of his historic position. In exile he produced book after book, a brilliant series of works unmatched in our time that, even more than the example of his life, remain the legacy of future generations. And you cannot drive a pickaxe into ideas.

Trotsky, the writer, would endure with a literary legacy in defiance of the silence of history. Farrell contended that Trotsky towered above American political theorists, especially by virtue of his powers of prediction. He pointed to the seriousness with which Trotsky confronted and held ideas. Trotsky's continual defense of dialectical materialism, Farrell remarked, was a personal concern and not related to matters of power. But there was also a "pragmatist" in Trotsky that Farrell claimed to see:

> For Trotsky, all intellectual ideas were practical and complete. His test for the validity of ideas was how they worked out in practice, in the actual framework of history. In this respect, he was close to the pragmatists. While Trotsky upheld some dogmas and was sometimes even schematic in his thinking, he was a relativist in his handling of ideas. He had an acute sense of the involvement of events in each other, of their interrelationships. I recall how, during the course of a disagreement with him, he emphasized the necessity of conceiving of a fact not merely as something which exists but also as something which is in process of becoming. This sense of becoming in events, of the relational character of events to each other, was one of his most remarkable intellectual traits. He never isolated political events; he saw them consistently in their international setting. He was no crude empiricist, nor did he indulge in easy psychological interpretations as a substitute for objective analysis. Some of us thought that our general theories were at times more sound than Trotsky's. We even took delight in proof that his philosophical formulations were

not modern and could easily be refuted through logical analysis. Yet Trotsky was more creative with his bad epistemology than we were with our good epistemology.

Farrell conveyed the different components of Trotsky's personality: his sharp contentiousness, as well as his warm, simple and charming grace. Additionally, there was Trotsky's self-discipline:

> ... Trotsky was unsparing of himself, subordinating all his impulses to his central purpose. I have never known another man whose very organism was so completely under the control of his will and intelligence.

Perhaps as a reminder of the task awaiting him in combatting the new prowar intellectuals, Farrell noted:

> One of Trotsky's traits that I admired most was his capacity for contempt. He knew how to despise those liberal intellectuals who, behind a set of pretentious gestures, invariably reflected the hypocrisy of bourgeois public opinion.

And finally:

> Some have been disconcerted by Trotsky's optimism and faith. But this faith, even if one cannot share it, is easily understood when one considers that they are necessary elements in any practical activity. What was to him a series of practical issues, was to his intellectualistic critics purely a set of formal questions. In formal intellectual activity we are not optimistic and believing but skeptical; and in some of Trotsky's theoretical opponents this skepticism sometimes results in irresponsibility. While he was risking his life for his ideas, they are risking a syllogism.

> Neither Stalinism nor the capitalist world can forgive Leon Trotsky. They will hate his memory, but they will never succeed in erasing it. History will know how to preserve it.

One of the best tributes we can pay to Trotsky is to understand him. These notes are an effort toward such an understanding. I offer them in tribute to the memory of the Old Man.

Farrell absorbed from Trotsky inspiration and strength, qualities he would especially require in the coming decade. The left intellectuals opposed to the new war were reduced to a handful. They included Farrell, Meyer Schapiro, Mary McCarthy, Edmund Wilson (in secluded retreat), Clement Greenberg, Dwight Macdonald and the pacifists grouped around *Politics,* C. Wright Mills, some Social Democrats, and the few who remained in the Trotskyist parties (such as Novack, Morrow, and the young Irving Howe). In addition to personal harassment for this unpopular stance, Farrell's fiction was continually subject to reprobation not only from the prowar Stalinist-liberal Popular Front, but also from censors in the federal government, Chicago (1944) and Philadelphia (1948). (One unexpected attack, and an unusually ignorant one, was conducted by Edmund Wilson in the *New Republic* at the start of the 1940s. Wilson took Farrell to task for a book he had not fully read; Farrell answered Wilson in the same issue with a powerful vindication of his aesthetic use of the functional concept of character, concrete processes, and the instrumentality of social institutions.) [8]

Additionally, the 1940s was a decade of personal tragedies for Farrell: the death of his mother; the birth of a retarded son (his first son, Sean, had died at the age of five days); the dissolution of his second marriage; and a serious fire in his apartment in 1946, which destroyed manuscripts of two novels, an eighty-page study of Irish literature, a book on censorship, and most of the "Death Fantasy" sequence which had been omitted from the published version of *Judgment Day.*[9] Finally, the decade included a complete and bitter rupture between Farrell and both the Cannon and Shachtman groups with which he had had personal political ties for almost fifteen years.

The termination of Farrell's regular column in *Partisan Review* (and also the weakening of his once friendly ties to the editors) introduced 1941 on a sour note. The final installment of Farrell's "The Cultural Front" appeared at the end of 1940. (It was a critique of Mortimer J. Adler, who had recently attacked positivism; Farrell dubbed him a great obfuscator and fellow traveler of the Catholic Church.) [10] The next issue of *Partisan Review* printed a letter from Farrell stating that two members of the editorial board had requested that he alternate his regular column with another one by Dwight Macdonald, thereby reducing his contribution to three per year in the bimonthly journal. Farrell declared that this did not seem "worthwhile" to him and announced the discontinuation of his column altogether. Following Farrell's letter, the editors politely commented:

> We are very sorry that Mr. Farrell does not wish to write his column every other issue and we hope that occasions will soon arise when he will contribute again to *Partisan Review*. [11]

Farrell has also recalled that, at the time, the *Partisan Review* editors asked him who he would like to have review his next book—a request he resented and regarded as petty. Farrell believed he was being eased out of the mainstream of *Partisan Review* contributors, and after that time relations between Farrell and the editors steadily deteriorated. [12] Farrell remained firm in his opposition to the war and in his support of literary realism; *Partisan Review* was moving away from him in regard to both these matters.

A letter from Philip Rahv to Farrell dated March 18, 1941, insisted that there was no ill will involved in the episode of reducing his column. [13] William Phillips recollects that Farrell was never in the middle of the magazine and he was close to the editors only in the beginning. Farrell's primary contributions to *Partisan Review*, Phillips recalls, were in the earlier period—in the fight on a theoretical level against Stalinism. And it was Farrell's earlier fiction which they had felt was most important. [14]

Dwight Macdonald's recollection of the incident is most candid. He believes that the attitude *Partisan Review* took toward Farrell's column was representative of the editorial board's general feelings about and relations with Farrell. Farrell was a quite prominent figure in those days, and the *Partisan Review* editors did not have many famous persons writing for them at that time. The column in *Partisan Review*, Macdonald recalls, was Farrell's idea, and some editors who opposed it were unable to see any way of getting out of it. Some of them believed the column was flat and banal, but felt a moral sense about retaining it and were fearful of hurting Farrell. Finally, Macdonald believes, they invented an excuse to get rid of it.[15]

Farrell's only other contribution to *Partisan Review* in 1941 was the publication of a letter addressed to Frieda Kirchway, editor of the *Nation*. Farrell requested a refund for past subscription money because, in reading Louis Fischer's *Men and Politics*, he learned that the *Nation*'s foreign correspondent admitted to suppressing facts about the Moscow Trials:

> In light of Mr. Fischer's own admission, I feel I was defrauded by the *Nation*. I think that it is only fair and proper of you to return to me the money I spent in subscriptions to your magazine. I was paying for honest intellectual goods, and now I learn from Mr. Fischer, himself, that I was not getting these goods.[16]

In the fall of 1941 the initial Smith Act victims went to trial. The famous "Minneapolis Case" was the first peacetime federal prosecution for sedition in American history. Supporters of the indicted Trotskyists (of the Socialist Workers party) and the teamster unionists claimed that the trial was engineered by the Roosevelt administration as part of its war preparations.

In the spring of 1941, Daniel J. Tobin, head of the Teamsters International (as well as the Democratic Party Labor Committee), declared war on Trotskyist-influenced Teamster local 544. Based in Minneapolis, this union had spearheaded labor organization in the Northwest. Its leaders, while maintaining an aggressive struggle for better working conditions, had refused to support Roosevelt's policies as the United States rapidly approached entry into World War II.

Tobin moved to appoint a receiver with absolute powers over the union, and its four thousand members responded by voting to disaffiliate from Tobin's AFL organization and to accept a charter from the CIO. Two and a half weeks later, FBI agents raided the branch offices of the Trotskyist Socialist Workers party in St. Paul and Minneapolis, confiscating large quantities of socialist literature. On July 15, a federal grand jury handed down an indictment under the Smith Act (a piece of reactionary legislation which had been opposed by the AFL, CIO and ACLU). That fall, the jury came to a verdict of "not guilty" on the first count of the indictment (which charged a conspiracy to overthrow the government by violence and force); but on the second count (of advocating such actions), eighteen of the defendants were declared guilty. They were sentenced on December 8, 1941, the day war was declared against Japan. As George Novack recalled:

> The Civil Rights Defense Committee, organized to handle the case, carried the appeal through the Eighth Circuit Court, which sustained the convictions, up to the U.S. Supreme Court. The highest court three times refused to hear the petition of the eighteen . . . almost one hundred and fifty local unions, representing over five million workers, supported the work of the Civil Rights Defense Committee and its efforts to obtain presidential pardon for the eighteen. But they were forced to serve their full sentences.[17]

In the summer of 1941, George Novack sublet a house in St. Paul with Evelyn Reed—his second wife, who would later write several books on Marxist anthropology. It was there that the central leaders of the Socialist Workers party—James Cannon, V. R. Dunne, and Farrell Dobbs—mapped out their defense strategy for the case.[18] Soon after the arrests, Novack went East to make preparations for gaining public and legal support. After stopping to meet with Trotskyists in New York, Novack went to the Cape Cod summer residences of John Dos Passos, Carlo Tresca, and Margaret De Silver. Dos Passos and Tresca agreed to serve as vice-chairmen of the newly founded Civil Rights Defense Committee (CRDC), and Margaret De Silver agreed to help financially (as she had also done with the Dewey Commission). Novack then sailed to Martha's Vineyard and conferred with Roger Baldwin, head of the ACLU, and Arthur Garfield Hays, its general counsel. They committed legal and moral backing from their organization. Farrell, in Manhattan, agreed to become chairman of the CRDC, and Evelyn Reed took charge of the staff which carried out the daily organizational tasks. The national committee of the CRDC enlisted sponsors over the next several years, including Joseph Warren Beach, Warren K. Billings, John Chamberlain, John Dewey, W. E. B. DuBois, Waldo Frank, Clement Greenberg, Mark DeWolfe Howe, Margaret Marshall, F. O. Matthiessen, Mary McCarthy, William Phillips, Philip Rahv, James Rorty, Max Shachtman, Meyer Schapiro, Charles Rumford Walker, Edmund Wilson, and many others. The ACLU and Workers Defense League also gave official endorsements.

The Minneapolis Case was the most important civil liberties cause during World War II. Among labor endorsers were top officers of the Auto Workers, the Marine and Shipbuilding Workers, the Textile Workers, the ILGWU of the AFL, the Michigan and New Jersey State CIO councils, fifty-eight UAW locals, twenty-two steel locals, and hundreds of other unions. Liberal and labor publications carried stories from the first, although the major national and big city papers played down the case. The CRDC issued over two hundred thousand pamphlets and leaflets, mobilized thirty active local committees to promote its campaign and raised more than fifty thousand dollars to defray the costs of the case and aid the families of the defendants while they were behind bars.

During the first half of the 1940s, Farrell actively supported the Minneapolis defendants. He subsequently collaborated with the Trotskyists during the related Kelly Postal Case, and also in the protest against the revoking of the *Militant* newspapers' mailing rights. On September 15, 1941, Farrell, Dos Passos, Walker, De Silver and Tresca issued an emergency appeal for funds for the twenty-nine members of the Socialist Workers party and leaders of Motor Transport and Allied Workers Industrial Union Local 544-CIO (formerly Teamsters AFL) who were originally charged. Their statement declared:

This prosecution is doubly unprecedented. Never before in peace-time has the government invoked statutes punishing the mere expression of opinion as it is doing with the Socialist Workers Party. Nor have the Federal authorities ever so flagrantly intervened in a trade union dispute by instituting criminal proceedings against the members of one labor organization, the CIO, on behalf of another, the AFL.[19]

The fund plea was for seventy-five hundred dollars; by October 3, forty-eight hundred dollars had been raised in loans and contributions.

Although doctor's orders forced Farrell to play a formal role at first,[21] the difference in commitment between himself and Dos Passos was clear.[22] Dos Passos's support was sincere, but more sentimental than active. (It sprang for the most part from his fear of a revival of the Wilsonian repressions and Attorney General Palmer's "Red Raids.")[23] Farrell's personal letters, however, revealed a passionate concern with the details and implications of the case:

> The government has charged [he wrote to his sister, Helen] that no overt act is necessary to constitute a conspiracy, and in other words, you cannot express your opinion: this is in violation of the Bill of Rights. Also, the government prosecutor was guilty of a slip of the tongue in court that was most revealing: he admitted that one of the defendants in the case is Leon Trotsky. He even brought in, as part of the charges, that the defendants discussed buying a machine gun to protect Trotsky's home and life in Mexico City, as if that had anything to do with the case.[24]

Much of Farrell's collaboration involved writing, speaking, fund raising, and collecting new sponsors of the CRDC. A September 15, 1941 letter from Novack asked Farrell to speak in Chicago on his return from Hollywood, where he was spending two weeks as a film writer. It also emphasized that:

> Unlike the Trotsky Defense Committee, this time we are going to get some real support from the trade unions and particularly from the CIO locals. This makes a great deal of difference in a defense fight.[25]

On September 25, Novack wrote Farrell thanking him for composing the foreword to the new CRDC pamphlet. He also reported that among the first to accept membership on the National Committee of the CRDC were Dewey, Eastman, Rahv, Schapiro, and Shachtman. John Chamberlain, Novack said, wanted to delay joining until November for fear of creating prejudice against a *Fortune* article he was writing. Macdonald had refused to join because of disagreements with and suspicions about the Socialist Workers party.[26] On October 27, Novack sent Farrell, still in Hollywood, a copy of the finished CRDC pamphlet, and also discussed with him the suicide of one of the defendants, Grant Dunne.[27] On October 18 Novack wrote to Farrell about activities in Washington, D.C., the attempt to win CIO support, and he enclosed a report on Roger Baldwin's interview with Attorney General Biddle. He also informed Farrell that Edmund Wilson and Mary McCarthy had joined the National Committee, and he complimented a *New Republic* article on the case by Dan Eastman (who was Max Eastman's son and a former Trotskyist party member).[28] On December 15, Farrell sent a speech to a protest meeting at the Hotel Diplomat in New York City.[29] The following year, 1942, Farrell's involvement relaxed, although he performed services and kept in touch.[30]

Novack's personal letters to Farrell during the summer of 1942 are also noteworthy. By July of that year, Evelyn Reed and George Novack were located in Detroit. Novack was working seven days a week as a machinist for the Hudson Motor Company.[31] In lengthy letters of July 25 and August 8, Novack discussed the CRDC only briefly. He concentrated mainly on describing the attitude of the workers toward the war. He emphasized the contradiction between their patriotic sentiments on the one hand, and their distrust of employers and union officials on the other:

The net impression I receive is one of tremendous hopefulness. It is impossible to live and work with thousands of auto workers without feeling their colossal latent power, their native intelligence, their organizing ability, their determination to fight for their rights, for their democracy and for their organization. Even though they often do not know how to fight for their aims, nor under whose leadership to fight.

With substantial detail, Novack attempted to explain how the class position and instincts of the workers led them toward a political understanding that was in some ways more palpable than that expressed by the learned treatises of Dwight Macdonald and found in *Partisan Review*. Novack also wrote about Sherwood Anderson, emphasizing how his total identification with his characters had at first been a strength, but was then transformed into a limiting weakness. This led to a brief discussion of Hegel and the dialectic, an issue which was a point of dispute between them. (Novack was in total agreement with Trotsky's views, and had been subject to the charge of hyperorthodoxy by others, such as Meyer Schapiro, who had a greater tolerance for pragmatism.)[32]

On January 12, 1943, Carlo Tresca was assassinated, probably by fascists or antiunion Mafia gunmen, in New York City. Farrell's tribute to Tresca was printed on the front page of the Trotskyist *Militant*, along with an article by Felix Morrow.[33]

Also occurring around the turn of the year was an incident in which the Postmaster General attempted to deprive the *Militant* of its second-class mailing rights because it allegedly

. . . discouraged participation in the war by the masses of the people. It is permeated with the thesis that the war is being fought solely for benefit of the ruling groups and will serve merely to continue the enslavement of the working classes.[34]

On February 2, 1943, a letter to the CRDC National Committee signed by Farrell and Novack reviewed the situation in light of the Post Office Department hearings on January 21 and called a meeting of the CRDC National Committee for February 9 to work out a protest strategy.[35] Farrell's statement was printed in the February 20th *Militant* on the front page.[36] The government's decision was soon reversed with the assistance of the ACLU.

This legal proceeding was followed by the Kelly Postal case, an outgrowth of the Minneapolis trials. Postal was one of the defendants against whom the original charges had been dismissed; but Tobin carried on a vendetta against Postal for his role in the disaffiliation of the local from the AFL. As Farrell explained in a letter to the *Nation:*

He [Postal] was indicted by the Hennepin County attorney for embezzlement. He was not accused of having misused funds personally. He was accused on this charge because, acting as treasurer of the local, he obeyed the democratic vote of the membership and transferred the union funds as he had been directed to.[37]

Farrell articulated his support of the Postal case in numerous public statements, and also contributed autographed books for fundraising raffles.[38] In a letter to Farrell, acknowledging a contribution for Postal and other funds Farrell had raised, Evelyn Reed declared:

I need hardly tell you how appreciative I am—not only because of the financial aid this gives us, but also because you are always so fully conscious of the value of publicizing our work. You are undoubtedly our best publicity agent.[39]

A month later, she added:

With all the work you have to do—you certainly do a lot for us! I am always surprised at where you find the time and energy.[40]

Farrell additionally released statements supporting the Minneapolis Eighteen when they were finally incarcerated, and he condemned the refusal of the Supreme Court to hear their appeal in early December 1943.[41] On December 26, 1943, Farrell was a guest speaker at a New York banquet in honor of the eighteen (who were about to go to jail).[42] Farrell also addressed a mass meeting at the Hotel Diplomat on February 2.[43] Throughout 1944, Farrell maintained his regular public statements demanding a pardon for the prisoners.[44] Farrell also continued collaboration with the CRDC—he donated money for literature for Felix Morrow to read in prison and made other small contributions regularly; he also gathered new endorsers for the CRDC.[45] Farrell's support was appreciated by the prisoners. On January 10, 1944, James Cannon wrote in a statement for publication:

The library here [at Sandstone prison] is small but there are enough books in it to keep me occupied for a while.

James T. Farrell will be pleased to learn that five of his books are here in the library. Only one was available, however. The rest are out—in the hands of other readers in our community.[46]

Following George Novack's April 1944 visit to Sandstone, Cannon wrote to his wife, Rose Karsner:

We all noted with satisfaction that George was looking very well, as though he is thriving on his arduous labors on our behalf. His work is deeply and genuinely appreciated by the comrades here. They speak of him very warmly, as they do also of the chairman of the Committee [Farrell]. I remarked in my polemic against [James] Burnham that worker-militants are very appreciative of intellectuals and only ask of them that they observe the excellent Arabian proverb: Shoot straight and tell the truth.[47]

Farrell wrote weekly to Felix Morrow at Sandstone, who was engaged in a "disciplined program of physical labor" (serving on the rock pile), literary reading, and the study of French.[48]

Farrell's strong convictions about the case were voiced in "Our Fight to Free the Eighteen," his preface to a collection of biographies of the prisoners. Farrell labelled the Minneapolis Labor case "the major case of the present war period involving the rights of labor and freedom of speech." He noted that the Smith Act was a "flat contradiction" of the Bill of Rights. Farrell warned:

The menace involved in these actions by the government and the federal courts should be clearly seen by all who have concern with the rights of labor and of freedom of speech. The history of fascism teaches us that the first attacks made by reaction are against the labor movement, and usually against its extreme left wing. The 18 prisoners in the Minneapolis Case belong to the Socialist Workers Party and to Minneapolis Truck Drivers local 544-CIO. As their indictments specifically state, they have been put behind bars because they propagate the ideas of Marx, Lenin and Trotsky, because they believe in the principles of the *Communist Manifesto.*

Now the force of law and the police power of the state, instead of reason, argument and debate, have become weapons used to combat the ideas of these defenders of Marxian socialism. Whether or not one agrees with the program and perspectives of this working-class political movement, it cannot be denied that Marxian socialists have consistently been in the forefront of the struggle for the advancement of labor and the defense of democratic rights. . . .

This attack upon labor, this suppression of socialist ideas and imprisonment of socialists paves the way toward fascist reaction even if it is taken by a government which proclaims itself the enemy of fascism. . . .[49]

Although the 1940s would end with Farrell's reevaluation of many of the fundamental political ideas to which he had devoted the mature years of his life, there was no hint of an apostasy in the early part of the decade. While the majority of Farrell's fellow radical intellectuals withdrew from the anticapitalist battleground—even in the area of defending basic civil liberties—Farrell only grew stronger and more courageous. As will be further demonstrated, his record of activities in defense of labor and civil liberties during World War II was augmented by political polemics similar to those of Randolph Bourne, the World War I dissident who had been the hero of the left intellectuals of Farrell's generation.

6.

The Lonely Decade

Napoleon had died in bitter exile on St. Helena. Waves must have smashed against the stones of that island lost in an ocean of water and an ocean of history; and the winds must have screamed across St. Helena as though in literal mockery.

Napoleon had heard many winds loud with the rage of ocean storms, but their vehemence and shattering roar had only been the shame of the silence of history.

James T. Farrell, *The Silence of History* [1]

In addition to writing fiction and engaging in Civil Rights Defense Committee activities, Farrell championed two causes during the war years: First, within the radical left he campaigned for a clear-cut antiwar/anticapitalist position; and second, he denounced and rebutted what he believed to be reactionary literary tendencies of the prowar intellectuals. Farrell's personal correspondence tends to display the first preoccupation, and his public articles the latter.[2]

In early 1942, Farrell pointed out in a letter to his publisher, James Henle, the necessity of writers taking the offensive against the dangerous mood of cultural witch-hunting being whipped up by the Stalinists and their liberal war allies (like Van Wyck Brooks).[3] Cultural conservatism, Farrell feared, was penetrating so deep that it was even affecting the one-time Marxists around *Partisan Review*. In one of several important letters to Meyer Schapiro in the summer of 1942, Farrell stated his fears about the increasing hostility of *Partisan Review* toward literary realism, and the editors' excessive absorption in certain aspects of Henry James' works:

> Many of the critics, etc., are really attacking it [realism] for concealed reasons. They want to substitute politeness for vigor in writing: they want to turn literature into the mirror reflecting their own anemic souls: when they talk of imagination, they limit the meaning of the term to the creation of myths, metaphors, and to the general confusing of confusion. . . . Many of them like Henry James because James is timid: because James can look at every reflection of an object without seeing the object: because he can go all around an impression, and so hedge that impression in qualifications that it becomes the shadow, and the shadow of the shadow of an impression.

> . . . the main point of my criticism is that they don't, and they didn't and can't create the right atmosphere around the magazine [*Partisan Review*]. They began by conceiving of an alliance between the independent radical intelligentsia, and the Southern Confederacy, etc. The former represented ideas; the latter represented culture. They are a cultural magazine with an overtone of radical ideas.[4]

Yet, as a revolutionary intellectual, where was Farrell to stand and with whom?

In a previous letter to Schapiro, Farrell had criticized his Trotskyist friends George Novack and Felix Morrow, two of the left intellectuals with whom he had much in common politically.

Certainly his criticisms of these two were fewer than those he levelled against the *Partisan Review* literati, but they were nevertheless substantial. In a letter to Farrell, Schapiro had expressed admiration for Novack "for having decided to give himself fully to revolutionary work." Yet Schapiro also detected "a humorlessness and a smugness in his 100% partisanship that I fear." Perhaps at bottom, Schapiro speculated, Novack and Morrow had inner doubts about the self-sacrifices they had made. Schapiro, especially, believed that Novack's reliance on the metaphor from Trotsky—that a "scratch" of deviation from the orthodox can produce a "gangrenous" revisionism—seemed to reinforce a proclivity toward fanatical orthodoxy.[5]

Farrell began by expressing partial sympathy with some of Novack's concerns:

> . . . the world of the petit bourgeois intellectuals is full of poisonous fluids. It is a world of people who sway with the winds, who talk rather than act. . . . Those closest to the revolutionary movement are often the most dangerous. . . . Their closeness is a kind of need in their lives. They have to earn their living doing things they hate, and in the earning of their bread, they have to handle the stale bourgeois values of the day. A sympathy for revolutionary values compensates them. But it remains a sympathy, one which is rather a feverish sympathy, and its temperature rises and declines in accordance with outside events. Unable to do more than retain this feverish sympathy, they bend to opinion, and as a kind of saving of their own faces, when they look in the mirror at themselves, they adopt the attitude that politics is a matter of personalities. They have a crying need to remark that Novack is pious; that Morrow is rude; that Shachtman is something of a clown. If these men didn't have such traits, such traits would have to be invented. . . . They have an effect of dragging discussions, ideas, everything important in this life down to banalities, down to personalities. This the real scratch becoming gangrene that George fears. . . .

Yet Farrell acknowledged that mere appeals to orthodoxy offered no solution:

The revolutionary intellectual has upon himself the duty of dealing in ideas in such a way that they will become a means of expanding horizons: in brief, that they will be made functional, that the background of ideas, attitudes, spiritual resources for social change is prepared. Culture to the nonrevolutionary intellectuals becomes more and more of an ornament.[6]

Despite what appeared to be the admirable devotion of their lives, Farrell was skeptical that Novack and Morrow were achieving what the historical period required. Farrell, in some ways like Schapiro, felt primarily tied to the Trotskyist movement through Trotsky (although Schapiro did not collaborate actively with Trotskyist parties as did Farrell).

Born in 1904 in Shavly, Lithuania, Schapiro arrived in the United States in 1907 and was naturalized in 1914. He finished his B. A. at Columbia in 1924, as an art history major, and received his doctorate in the early 1930s. Remaining on the Columbia faculty during and after the thirties, Schapiro broke early with the Communists (around the same time as the *Menorah Journal* group), and joined Sidney Hook and others attempting to unite anti-Stalinist radicals during the 1930s. Although the Socialist Workers party did not attract Schapiro as an organization, he had a number of friends who were in or close to the party and he often read its publications.[7] And even as the 1930s ended and the 1940s began, Schapiro retained a tremendous admiration for Trotsky. In the summer of 1942, Schapiro wrote to Farrell:

Most important is what you tell me of Leon Trotsky's book which I want very much to read. If it were here, I would stop everything to read it from cover to cover in one sitting; that is how I read him in the past.[8]

In a letter of July 25, 1942, Schapiro had explained:

I share your enthusiasm for Trotsky's *My Life;* I read it in two sittings when I was a student in the graduate school, and it gave me the deep respect for Leon Trotsky that I have preserved to this day. His attackers remind me of Shake-speare's "water-flies, diminutives of nature," in *Troilus and Cressida* (a fine play, with criticisms of the Greek heroes, that you should read). What is so wonderful about Leon Trostsky is that he kept to the last day the same heroic energy and devotion, he never gave out. . . .[9]

Farrell's response was in accord:

What happens with me is the same concerning L. D. [Trotsky]. Once I pick up one of his books, I slight all other readings to go ahead with him, and that is what I have been doing. I've almost finished it, and after tonight, I can read other things again. . . .

But Farrell's letters to Schapiro were by no means confined to political discussion. He could also suddenly slip into rumination about the dark mysterious core of his artistic self, a writer who ultimately must face the world and society alone, at night, with only his pen and his mind:

. . . underlying everything else in life, there is the biological tragedy of man. In *Father and Son*, I tried to write of this, for Jim's tragedy was, even more than the social tragedy of man, the biological one, and it filled my mind for a long time: in fact, it made me morbid. It was at that time that I developed high blood pressure—Jim [the character based on Farrell's father] had it—and I noticed myself beginning to drink heavily.[10]

Nevertheless, this dark inner aspect of Farrell, his preoccupation with the biological tragedy, was only one part of his self-concept and was voiced almost exclusively in his art. His literary criticism, in contrast, tended to emphasize his capacity as a revolutionary Marxist intellectual; and a few months after such a personal expression of emotion to Schapiro, Farrell's correspondence with a Trotskyist union militant, V. R. Dunne, showed a lively enthusiasm for workers' education.[11]

If anything, Farrell's Marxist convictions seemed to harden as his isolation increased and as the switch of quondam radical intellectuals to support of the war became more overt and numerous. This was especially displayed in two letters to John Switalski in April 1943. No doubt Farrell thought of Trotsky and how he bore his exile, as he himself stood increasingly alone. And within Farrell arose that "contempt" he admired in Trotsky, as he surveyed what he saw as the retreat of John Dos Passos, Max Eastman, Sidney Hook, and the majority of the *Partisan Review* editors, along with the limitations of the radical pacifism of Dwight Macdonald. The first letter to Switalski affirmed Farrell's admiration for classical Marxist thinkers, and it explained that he had devoted considerable time to re-examining them since the war began. Farrell's assessment of Lenin was clear and striking:

Lenin is endless as a source of encouragement, as a guide, as one to study. His analyses are unrivaled in acuteness: I refer to his writings on the First World War, during it. Lenin never allowed a difference of opinion to go unanalyzed. That is the way a scientist works. He investigates every variation. That is what the bourgeois world really means when they call him a fanatic. I am reading *Materialism and Empirio-Criticism* now. I was wrong in dismissing it before. He is basically right against Mach and the idealists in insisting on the objectivity of the object. . . . You must read Lenin's writings during the First World War. They are among the most important of his writings, and they are important to read in this period. Again and again, I have gone to them and gained a kind of consolation and encouragement during the dark days of this War.

Reflecting on the genius of Lenin and Trotsky, Farrell underscored particularly the early age at which Trotsky had written imposing works and outlined theoretical conceptions. Farrell concluded that "in revolutionary periods, in times of growing ferment, youth learns quickly." He cited St. Just and Napoleon as further examples. Farrell additionally urged Switalski to undertake an organized study of Marx's *Capital:*

Do a little each week. In time, you will see the results of this. I'm doing this now in reading all of Aristotle.[12]

In a second letter, a few weeks later, Farrell criticized Sidney Hook and Dwight Macdonald. Farrell was perturbed because a recent article by Hook in *Partisan Review* had argued (in Farrell's paraphrase) "that it is cowardly to take an antiwar position and sane and brave to take his [Hook's prowar] position, and that science is behind you if you do." Farrell had learned that Macdonald was giving Hook space in *Politics,* and he found it "inexcusable that he [Macdonald] should allow Hook to turn the whole symposium into an abusive attack on the weak left." Farrell quoted from a letter Trotsky wrote to Albert Goldman, in which he asserted that Macdonald's notion of "scepticism toward all theories, faith in the revolutionary masses," was "nothing but preparation for personal desertion." Macdonald's kind of devotion, Trotsky had argued,

> is impossible without theoretical understanding of the laws of this revolutionary fight. Revolutionary devotion is possible only if one gains the assurance that his devotion is reasonable, adequate; that it corresponds to its aims. Such assurance can be created only by theoretical insight into the class struggle.[13]

Even more reprehensible, Farrell thought at the time, was the role of Sidney Hook:

> Hook is playing a Kautsky role, that of mediating professorially between groups, trying to stand above them on the mountain of theory and science, looking down, handing out bouquets and criticisms, justifying desertions with pretenses of objective scientific appreciation, telling everyone that the real left is merely lunatic, infantile, and so on, and dealing it another hard blow when it is small, isolated, persecuted.[14]

Three letters to Meyer Schapiro in June 1943 show that the switch of many left intellectuals from antiwar to prowar positions, against which both Farrell and Schapiro had polemicized, only served to strengthen Farrell's upholding of Marx, Lenin, and Trotsky. Furthermore, it was partially the present turn of events that inspired Farrell to attempt to tell the story of the New York intellectuals in fictional form, through the Bernard Carr novels. On June 5, Farrell discussed in detail his negative reaction to Hook's retort to Schapiro (in the *Partisan Review* debate about the war, triggered by Hooks's essay "The New Failure of Nerve").[15] Farrell declared his contempt for what he considered to be backsliders like Hook and Eastman, and appended several more names to the list of those he suspected to be making their peace with capitalism: Elliot Cohen, Herbert Solow, and William Phillips. Then, returning to Hook, Farrell pointed to limitations inherent in restricting oneself to John Dewey's philosophy:

> Deweyism has long since passed its zenith as an inspirational philosophy for young men, and it can safely be predicted that with the war, etc., there will be no new generations marching out of the colleges as inspired by Deweyism as was that of Randolph Bourne. Sidney will not get very far with Deweyism. . . .

> I was interested in your further comments on Dewey. I agree— he is really basically complacent about America. I think that in his earlier books you'll find the same strain of thought and attitude.[16]

Indeed, it seemed as if Farrell's revulsion at Hook's transformation, and at Hooks' apparent influence on Macdonald, impelled Farrell toward an orthodox Trotskyist discussion of the need for a Leninist party:

> Dwight has never seriously studied and thought about the organizational question: he has picked up on the current criticisms of Lenin's organizational ideas, and added to that, there is his experience in the Trotskyist movement. He says more democracy, and lets the matter rest there. Luxemburg had no party, and therefore, she could not manage a necessary retreat, and the revolution was drowned in blood. Lenin had a

party: he was able to manage a necessary retreat in the July days. This is always forgotten by the critics of Lenin. Further, there is a functional relationship between a revolutionary party and the society in which it exists. It suffers from the weaknesses of its society. This business of talking about needing new ideas, a new party, etc., is all empty unless it is concrete, demonstrative in showing what is meant, what is the new organization, what are the new ideas. Further, Dwight says that the new party should appeal to more than the workers—intellectuals, etc. The working class is not enough; it can't win alone. But it is not clear—should the working class element compromise with the petit bourgeois element, or should it drag the petit bourgeois element along by decisive action, clear programme, etc.? [17]

One consequence of Farrell's intense examination of those intellectuals around him was that the concept behind the original Bernard Carr project began to emerge:

I was talking with George [Novack], about N.Y. life, the twenties, and so on. He remarked on how so many—how he, for instance—came to N.Y., wanting to be a business success and a great philosopher—how [Clifton] Fadiman wanted to be rich and also a great literary critic, how most young men who read, etc., came to N.Y. in the 20's to make a fortune as well as fame—stating that this was a fundamental contradiction in them. I see this as so and want to make it concrete and clear in the book.

Reminiscing about his own development, Farrell noted that he had largely extricated himself from this contradiction (of wanting artistic fame and also money) in college, although he brought his gigantic literary ambitions with him to New York when he first came in 1927:

Thinking of N.Y. in those days, I realize thousands of boys girls came here to become the great American actor and actress, to write the great American novel, play, poem, to become the great American philosopher, to conduct the great American advertising campaign—to become the great American something or other. George described New York in those days as a suction pump, drawing and sucking the most intelligent, spirited and adventurous boys and girls of all America here ... it was New York that was the magnet. Ambitions were poured into this city. And what happened to them? Here is one of the main things I must develop, discover, correlate, and put down in concrete ways in terms of character. . . .

The story I am trying to do [the Bernard Carr series] is really the story of the petit bourgeois intellectual, and the cause of the degeneration, spending of talents, perversion, debasing and shifting of the outlet for these talents is really the story of what capitalism does to the petit bourgeois class.

... Another point. The characters in the book never realize that they change drastically. What happens is that the world changes: they are betrayed by history; the masses have let them down; Stalin has murdered the revolution. And that is the change; but they generally do not sense themselves as changing.

Farrell also discussed some unique features that differentiated himself, Schapiro, and some others from the mass of young hopefuls who, in the Bernard Carr series, would be unprepared for the Depression and new war, and swept, with their ambitions, into either the Stalinist or commercial-cultural stream:

Also, George was remarking on the pacifism of those days. The number of youths who said from [19]26 on—it will never happen again. Again, this is not quite parallel to my own case. From 26 on, I was convinced that it would happen again. I assume that your own experiences, your own attitudes, etc., were far from the norm here, not only because you were more developed than most of those your age, but also because background, experience as a YPSL [Young Peoples Socialist

League], etc. Sidney [Hook], the same, I would assume. There was a sense of the labor and revolutionary movement which most of those who came here lacked.[18]

From the beginning of the 1940s, Farrell meticulously surveyed the political events at home and abroad, sometimes rising to heights of passion in his correspondence:

> I just got the latest news over the radio and read the afternoon papers [he wrote to John Switalski]. It leaves me so excited that I find it difficult to work. There can be no doubt left but that the revolution has started in Italy, and that it seems to be spreading very rapidly. The latest news indicates that in Milan, which is the center of events, the power is now in the streets and if the workers are not in control of Milan, they are so damned close to control that it almost amounts to the same thing.[19]

In addition, Farrell maintained relations with figures from the international revolutionary movement:

> Alfred Rosmer and I were good friends and comrades, and had considerable correspondence.

> I am mentioned and quoted three times by Christian Gras in his book on Alfred. Alfred sent me inscribed copies of his books. I saw much of him in New York, and in Paris, in 1938, in 1949 and the Fifties. I last saw him in Paris in 1956.

> I met Walter Held and a few of the other Trotskyites a couple of times in 1938.

> I might have met Pierre Naville then. I met him in New York about 1946 or 1947. I talked with him mainly about his book on Saint Teresa of Lisieux, the Little Flower of Jesus, which I had read in French.

> I never met Victor Serge. But I once collected twenty five dollars from a woman, of vague Stalinist sympathies, in

Hollywood to be sent to Victor Serge in Mexico in order that he could buy a gun with which to protect himself, because he was afraid of Stalinist assassination attacks.

I met Boris Souvarine in Paris in 1938, and we are friends to this day. I last saw him in Paris in 1972.

Two of the first books that I ever read in French were Alfred Rosmer's *Le Movement Ouvrier pendant la Guerre,* and Boris's [Souvarine's] *Staline.*

Farrell also corresponded with Natalia Trotsky, whom he considered to be one of the greatest women of the twentieth century.[20]

However, it was Farrell's literary criticism in the 1940s which most exhibited his relentless struggle to create new revolutionary perspectives for writers and intellectuals. The groundwork for Farrell's main attack was mapped out in three published articles during 1941 and 1942: "The Faith of Lewis Mumford," "On the 'Brooks-MacLeish Thesis,' " and "Literature and Ideology." It was then summarized in "The Frightened Philistines" in late 1944.[21] The thesis of these writings was that the prowar intellectuals of the 1940s were analogous to those who capitulated to World War I. With reference to a passage in the *Communist Manifesto,* which explained how the bourgeoisie demeaned the professional occupations, Farrell ridiculed the naiveté of those literati who had "Enlightenment illusions of a free market for cultural productions" in capitalist society. To the contrary, Farrell noted, the tendency had been for the number of independent artists to diminish and increasingly resemble wage laborers. Now, with the onset of the war, a certain grouping of critics and book reviewers were mobilizing sentiment especially against those writers who had taken risks to keep themselves independent; and these were writers who tended to be rebels in the realistic or experimental genres. Van Wyck Brooks, for example, had accused Farrell, Faulkner, Hemingway, and Dos Passos of being destructive to civilization, because of their alleged lack of faith in the family, lack of roots in the soil, and disparagement of the dignity of man. Brooks claimed that these realist and experimentalist writers helped to demoralize the American nation so it would be unable properly to fight Hitler.

In response, Farrell especially propounded the social worth of literary realism, pointing out that realist writers were the ones who "assessed the cost of bourgeois society in terms of what happens to people." Farrell also wrote in support of cultural iconoclasts like James Joyce, Marcel Proust, Charles Baudelaire and Arthur Rimbaud, defending their experimentalism against all "ideological policemen" and "sheepherders of the status quo." Quoting Karl Marx, Randolph Bourne and Leon Trotsky, Farrell polemicized against the pro-war intellectuals, whom he dubbed "The League of Frightened Philistines." Mobilizing the power of his contempt, he charged that the pro-World War II intellectuals were in truth more reactionary than those of World War I: " . . . struggling to express a faith to justify a new war in defense of democracy, they abandon what is best in democracy."

The essay "Literature and Ideology" exposed the similarity between the views of the prowar intellectuals and the Stalinist attempt to judge literature by political criteria in the early 1930s (which, Farrell repeatedly charged, actually destroyed the creative output of a number of writers). Some who opposed the Stalinists' earlier exploitation of literature for immediate political ends now supported the new abuses. Reemphasizing the thesis of *A Note on Literary Criticism,* Farrell questioned whether formal ideology should really be the key to evaluating art. Literature recreates the consciousness of a period, Farrell affirmed, and just as science helps humankind understand nature, so literature helps human beings understand themselves. Throughout the essay, Farrell used formulations and phrases which seemed to echo some of Trotsky's manifestos on culture and other writings:

Farrell:
"Literature generally reflects life. It often limps, even crawls, behind events."

Trotsky:
"The nightingale of poetry, like that bird of wisdom, the owl, is heard only after the sun is set. . . . As a matter of fact, all through history, mind limps after reality."

Farrell:

"Literature by its very nature, cannot, in and of itself, solve social and political problems. Any solution of a social or political problem in a work of literature is a purely intellectual solution. These problems are problems of action."

Trotsky:

"To find a solution to this impasse through art itself is impossible. . . . Art can neither escape the crisis nor partition itself off. Art cannot save itself. . . . The task is essentially revolutionary in character." [22]

One of Farrell's polemics on the prowar intellectuals produced an additional altercation with Max Eastman, whom Farrell had criticized in passing. A few months later in a public exchange in the pages of *Partisan Review,* Eastman tried to justify his position in the 1940s of rejecting socialism as being consistent with his past values. These values, Eastman argued, had never changed; it was the facts which had proven the "Marxian hypothesis" to be false. Furthermore, the facts showed that the intellectuals' central responsibility at present was to defend the level of civilization already achieved, and this accomplishment would surely be "destroyed, by a transfer of all power and industry to a revolutionary state, whether it calls itself proletarian or fascist." Eastman continued:

The real difference between us [Eastman, Corey, Hook, Dos Passos, etc.] and you, in my opinion, is this: in a period when certain means we had all agreed upon for emancipating the working class and therewith all society, have proven to lead in the opposite direction, we have remained loyal to the aim, you to the means. . . . You do not care that much about the workers or about human freedom. You care more about your own emotional and intellectual life which had been organized around the means.

Eastman charged that in private conversation Farrell had voiced doubts about the dictatorial aspects of revolution, and had even admitted that "It makes one hesitate to summon the workers to revolution." Furthermore, Eastman claimed that Farrell's article ("On the 'Brooks-MacLeish Thesis,' " in *Partisan Review*) unjustifiably amalgamated him with Brooks and employed some "gross inventions" which placed it "morally and intellectually on a level with the Moscow Trials." Finally, Eastman pleaded with Farrell to break with the "nearsighted cranks and crosspatchers, the wounded veterans of an exploded theology," and help build a "new radical movement . . . based on a straightout recognition that Marxism is unscientific and complete collectivism a failure."

Farrell replied to Eastman by arguing that the former revolutionist had made unwarranted amalgams himself. The first one was Eastman's placing himself within a diverse group that included people like Louis Hacker and Sidney Hook, who had been attacking each other; and the second one was his treatment of Farrell as representative of another group:

> It is doubtful whether or not some members of this group would even say hello to one another. . . . It is well known to readers of this magazine that the editorial board of *Partisan Review* is split on the war question. One of the editors, Philip Rahv, is decidedly more in agreement with Max Eastman on the war than he is with either Dwight Macdonald or myself. While Macdonald and I are in agreement concerning the position that socialism is the only solution to the problems posed by contemporary society, we do not agree on the character of fascist economy. The Trotskyist movement is split, and both wings of it attack *Partisan Review*.

Besides, how could Eastman possibly claim that he had not changed his values? Once he defended the basic program of socialism, and now he opposed it. Once Eastman criticized Marxist methodology in order to "liberate" it from German metaphysics; now he labeled it a danger to human freedom.

Point by point Farrell answered Eastman's newly announced

views. If, as Eastman claimed, the degeneration of the Russian Revolution proved the impossibility of a socialism, then why didn't the defeat of bourgeois democracy vis-à-vis fascism in country after country prove that capitalism must also be abandoned?

Farrell claimed that even more banal were Eastman's philosophical arguments, which in essence stated that humanity was ruled by instincts and that some of these instincts made it impossible to establish a socialist society. Not only did this fly in the face of the work of Pavlov, C. Judson Herrick, Dr. Paul Schilder, and Freud, but against

> the social psychology of such American pragmatists as John Dewey and the late [George] Herbert Mead. And in passing, I might add that there are footnotes in the first volume of Marx's *Capital* which anticipate and imply Mead's idea of the social basis of personality. While Karl Marx never anticipated MacDougal [an instinct psychology theoretician], he did anticipate the work of many contemporary psychologists, social workers, and others who seriously study the phenomenon of alienation in our society.

Ultimately Farrell explained that he was not guilty of making an amalgam between Eastman and Brooks at all, but rather that he had indicated a parallel:

> I was far from unmindful of Max Eastman's well-known views on art when I described him as a Philistine. In the field of literature, he has been consistently conventional in theory, in taste, and in practice. A number of his literary ideas are too banal to merit discussion. He has been continually unsympathetic to most new work. He has written of literary radicals in the same kind of abusive language that one always finds in the "criticism" of literary Philistines. Eastman's rambunctiously literal-minded attacks on the "cult of unintelligibility" (such writers as James Joyce, T. S. Eliot, E. E. Cummings and Hart Crane) paved the way for the later moralistic abuse which Van Wyck Brooks has poured on these men.[23]

Farrell's literary criticism of the 1940s was primarily concerned with the following: the role of the revolutionary writer and intellectual; the extension of Marxist theory to understanding literature; reviews of various new books; a series of evaluations of classic novels. Yet, as Farrell remarked in the preface to *The League of Frightened Philistines* (a 1946 collection which brought together many of his past articles), the unity of such writings was due to their expressing "a constant struggle for a clearer perspective and a better orientation." (Again, Farrell seemed to echo Trotsky, who wrote: "Art, culture, politics needs a new perspective. Without it humanity will not develop.") [24] The imposing role of Meyer Schapiro as an intellectual stimulator was also acknowledged by Farrell in the introduction to the collection:

> The greatest [debt] is to Professor Meyer Schapiro of Colum-
> bia University. I have had many discussions and extensive
> correspondence with him, some relating to the writers and
> problems treated in some of these papers; some concerning
> French culture, and also the nineteenth century idea of
> seeking freedom in culture. Besides, I attended a series of
> lectures he gave on nineteenth-century and modern French
> painting. From all, I absorbed much.[25]

Bernard Clare, published the following year, was dedicated "To Lillian and Meyer Schapiro."

The essays in *The League of Frightened Philistines,* as well as in *Literature and Morality* (1947) and a number of uncollected pieces (many of which have unfortunately been ignored for two and a half decades), constitute a striking chapter in the effort of American left-wing intellectuals to employ a Marxist method in probing the functions of literature in society and the role of the writer in the process of changing human consciousness.

In this light, it might at first seem difficult to explain the scathing attack launched against Farrell as a writer and critic in late 1947 in *Partisan Review* by Irving Howe (himself a veteran of almost ten years in Marxist parties—first, briefly, the Socialist Workers party, and then, for most of the time, the Workers party). Provocatively called "The Critic Calcified," the review purported to survey Farrell's three published volumes on criticism (starting with *A Note on Literary Criticism*). However, only a few of Farrell's articles were mentioned. Howe's focus was on a defense of Lionel Trilling's story "The Other Margaret," and Isaac Rosenfeld's novel *Passage from Home*. (Farrell's review of this last work had not even been published in any of the three collections.) [26]

Howe issued a series of rather harsh indictments against Farrell to the effect that, in spite of his courageous upholding of "desirable values" as an "anti-Stalinist militant Marxist," Farrell's literary criticism was tantamount to sociological-ideological reductionism and mere moral censure. Inasmuch as this was precisely the kind of charge that Farrell had previously levelled at the Stalinists, it might appear that one of Howe's main critical goals would have been to demonstrate how and why Farrell fell into the very trap he had warned against. Yet, in his essay, Howe primarily marched along through the counts of the indictment, cataloging Farrell's limitations and omissions, declaring him a "moralistic Yvor Winters of the left." Howe also announced that Farrell's importance in American cultural life had become greater than his actual work warranted, and that Farrell's creative talents had declined since the Studs Lonigan trilogy.[27]

As objectively as one might try to read Howe's piece—especially considering that the young intellectual subsequently revealed himself as one of the major critical talents of his generation—I cannot avoid the following conclusion: Howe's arraignment is not just a severe criticism of this or that critical judgment made by Farrell, nor the mapping out of a pattern of methodological weaknesses, but a systematic demolition of the entire literary significance of James T. Farrell.

The context of this review was that Howe was in this period an intellectual in transition, moving from years as a literary-political journalist of the Workers party into becoming the socialist voice in the circle of New York intellectuals identified with *Partisan Review* and *Commentary* magazines. Although Farrell shared a certain tradition in the New York literary left with this circle, relations had become increasingly strained during the 1940s as Farrell saw many of these intellectuals abandoning their Marxism under the impact of the war, and turning away from the literary movements of realism and naturalism with which Farrell so firmly identified. Up until the point of his harsh review, it is likely that Howe was seen as an ally of Farrell, and it is possible that the publication of the piece marked a turning point in Howe's evolution.

In my opinion, the content of Howe's article strongly suggests that Howe was undergoing a substantial reassessment of some of his views in the process of integrating himself into the New York intellectual circle. It is to this factor that I am inclined to attribute what seem to be many unfair and injudicious claims in the review. Howe charges that Farrell did not "respect the medium in which he works" and that "He is not passionately convinced that a work of art is unique and irreducible." As I have tried to reveal in this study, the whole history of Farrell's years of literary struggle with Stalinist and commercial tendencies shows that, above all, it was precisely a "respect for the medium" (which Farrell inherited from the 1920s) which motivated his debates at every turn.[28]

This is not to say that Farrell's contributions to literary criticism were without significant limitations. His only book length work was a short polemic and not intended to be conclusive. Farrell hoped to develop and expand it, but never had the opportunity. Yet the record of his critical work does demonstrate a number of striking attempts to apply Marxist concepts, often as developed by Trotsky, to the study of culture and related matters. It is primarily because so much of Farrell's work was brief that there may be some grounds to charge "reductionism." When Farrell explained, for example, the role of money in *Sister Carrie*, the nonpolitical yet liberating impact of *The Sun Also Rises*, the frontier democratic current in Mark Twain, Irish nationalism in *Portrait of the Artist as a Young Man*, social forces in *The Brothers Karamazov*, and so on, he was emphasizing aspects of literature of special interest to Marxists (or which Marxists might consider important to highlight). He was expanding the conception of literary studies, broadening criticism out into its historical, political, economic, philosophical dimensions, and not primarily "reducing." Also, if Farrell is to be designated as a "moralist" in the 1930s and 1940s—and in any event, he carefully described his own notion of "social morality"[29]—it is to his credit that he was capable of demonstrating the positive contribution to cultural development made by writers whose personal views and philosophy he regarded as reactionary (Dostoyevski) and banal (Dreiser).

Unless one conceives of literary criticism as a kind of pure, supersocial exercise (which could hardly be a Marxist view), one of Farrell's strengths was precisely his ability to differentiate artistic judgments from polemics against the other views of the author, or even from the reactionary implications of a work itself. Farrell, like all critics, made errors in prediction and judgment; but the mainstream of his critical contribution (his evaluation of the 1930s fiction especially, as well as his essays on European and American classics) seems hardly controversial today.

Of course, Farrell was primarily a writer of fiction who believed he must search for truth through the penetration of common experiences and emotions. In certain areas he felt an affinity for Trotsky's intellect; for example, in his interest in the French revolutionary tradition and absorption of nineteenth-and twentieth-century Western European culture. But in Farrell such interests were tempered by an immersion in pragmatism and his unique struggle to release himself from Chicago's South Side cultural wasteland through art. However, in addition to its obvious presence as political inspiration, the refracted impact of Trotsky's Marxism is there in Farrell's critical thought and writing. It can particularly be felt in the contentiousness of his argument, the bold and often humorous use of metaphor, the respect and search for method and theory (with the goal of prediction), the political and cultural internationalism, the struggle to integrate all facets of human reality into one's work and to make that work consonant with one's life and beliefs (at all costs), and in Farrell's power of penetration to the social root and significance of human, historical, and cultural phenomena. Farrell's weaknesses and limitations were imposed largely by the specific circumstances of his intellectual origins, as was expressed by Murray Kempton's moving tribute:

> The poverty of the plebeian writer's environment follows him wherever he goes. Farrell once said that a writer's style is his childhood. . . .

he was, and would always be, received as a barbarian in the

genteel world of the literary supplements, just as Theodore
Dreiser had been, because poverty had blunted his fingertips
and left his work heavy with passion and deficient of
charm. . . .

The plebeian's survival was an act of the will almost from
the nursery. When Dreiser died, Farrell wrote him a farewell
that would have seemed bathos from anyone else; in Farrell, it
had some of the majesty of Dreiser's own mastery of the
cumulative cliché: "We have lost a man who made the way
easier for many of us. . . . His work encourages us to struggle.
. . . Farewell, Theodore Dreiser, you, creator of titans, were a
greater titan yourself." Farrell's world, like Dreiser's, was one
whose inhabitants understood the price the artist pays. They
looked at the New York literary world and thought it
commercial, supercilious, logrolling, and absolutely alien.[30]

The impressive range of Farrell's writings in the 1940s was an
extension of the versatility already demonstrated in his reviews of
the early 1930s.[31] "The Historical Image of Napoleon," which
Horace Gregory judged "One of the best historical essays in
twentieth century criticism," [32] contains a Marxist critique of
Tolstoy's theory of history.[33] A series of articles on Hollywood, the
significance of commercialization, and film culture, culminated in
the important "The Fate of Writing in America," which traced
centralization in publishing and linked it to growing Hollywood
trends. (This concern later became an important underlying theme
of Farrell's 1971 novel *Invisible Swords*.) [34]

Farrell's critiques of the Stalinists in the cultural field, generally
from the Trotskyist frame of reference, continued. Especially
incisive was Farrell's response to the literary dispute that followed
the expulsion of Earl Browder from the Communist party, which
Albert Maltz initiated in the pages of the *New Masses*. With
political acumen, Farrell demonstrated that the Communists'
recent cultural orientation of vague patriotism corresponded to
their wartime politics. So long as liberal prowar writers did not
attack the Stalinist party line directly, the party gave them a
certain latitude; and on occasion, for memory's sake, seasoned

party members, like Samuel Sillen and Howard Fast, made token references to Marxist theory. But after Browder's expulsion, a new left-wing political line was more clearly emerging at the very moment when Maltz had blundered into writing a call for "softening" up against political opponents like Farrell and Richard Wright! The basis of this new turn by the Communists was the need to create a radical-sounding political cover for Stalin's "nationalist expansionist" postwar program. Farrell used the articles he wrote on the intra-Stalinist debate to reaffirm that a substantial difference lay between the problems of literature and politics.[35]

"Social Themes in American Realism" described a shift in American fiction from an emphasis on personal consciousness (found in Henry James and others) to the Dreiserian revolution, where "characters take on coloration of the environment." Farrell demonstrated the influence of Populism and the growing thematic importance of the increase in leisure time and consumption during the 1920s (which culminated in Hemingway's world of tourists).[36]

In the September and October 1946 issues of *New International,* Farrell's two-part article, "American Literature Marches On," explicitly attempted to apply Marxist theoretical tools, and particularly the law of uneven and combined development. (Most fully developed by Trotsky, this theory deals with the different rates of growth among the various elements of social life.) Farrell explained the concept by using the example of Marx's method of abstraction in *Capital:* Marx had pictured, for the purpose of explication, a structure of pure capitalism operating without impediment. The law of uneven and combined development was meant as a corrective to a too literal application of such theoretical constructs; the law adjusts abstractions to the complexities of historical and social development. In this essay, Farrell treated the evolution of American literature as partially the story of how men and women had tried to live in a commodity civilization, and he maintained once more that serious American literary realism was the most highly-developed literary tool for understanding what happens to humankind under such conditions.[37]

In "The Politics of Psychoanalysis," Farrell attacked those who attempted to interpret Freudianism as a political trend, and he argued for its assimilation as a branch of medicine. He also indicated the way in which Freud's thought had served as a liberating influence in his own life.[38]

Farrell also contributed biographical and political portraits of two Irish working-class leaders, James Larkin and James Connolly, to the *New International.* Farrell had once met Larkin, and had discussed the Moscow Trials with him, and he offered a powerful eulogy calling Larkin the "great heart" of the proletariat. [39] The Connolly article, which extended over five issues, embodied a revolutionary call for labor to take the lead in the Irish liberation movement.[40]

A two-part series in the *Humanist* explored and developed a combination of themes regarding the danger of commercialism, the implications of Hollywood's Motion Picture Code, and the war hysteria. Farrell emphasized the difference between obligations to society and to the state; he charged that in the United States there were indications that criticism was drifting in the direction of becoming an instrument of the state. He warned against the danger of loyalty to abstractions—such as "democracy," "state," and "social consciousness"—without precise content; he showed how writers could lose their confidence as a result of the contradiction inherently posed by capitalism between integrity and financial success. Thus writers had fallen prey to simple formulas of liberalism and Popular Front Stalinism: They abstracted responsibility from their art and "fulfilled" it by adherence to a party or formula. In contrast, Farrell countered, the real obligation of the artist is the "pitiless exploration of the nature of experience."

The writer's responsibility, Farrell concluded, was to use freedom seriously: one function of art was the aesthetic and emotional experience it creates, but there was also a social importance in the work, inspiring the reader with the need for growth, knowledge, and change. Speaking openly as a socialist, Farrell affirmed the inspiration of Robespierre and the revolutionary Marxists and explained that the novel could awaken consciousness of revolutionary ideas by exploring the nature of experience.[41]

Farrell's political orientation did not remain static throughout the decade of the 1940s. Following the Moscow Trials, Farrell had gone through a phase of immersion in intensely personal fiction (especially about his father). In the early 1940s, under the threat of war's holocaust, he prepared himself politically by taking a more critical view of his intellectual allies on the anti-Stalinist left, and by reassessing and consolidating his revolutionary Marxism. Throughout the first six years of the decade his role as an ally of the Trotskyist movement seemed firm and consistent, although he kept his distance. According to George Novack, this relationship was to some degree mutually desirable:

> It was only once, in 1944, that he [Farrell] actually proposed to join [the Socialist Workers party]. It was mutually agreed almost from the beginning of our association that he was most valuable in polemicizing against the Stalinists and aiding our movement, as well as writing his works, if he remained unaffiliated.[42]

But toward the mid-1940s Farrell began to develop stronger differences with the Socialist Workers party led by Cannon. Farrell was not involved enough in internal party affairs to be an authentic part of a particular grouping, but he was affected by some of the same factors and concerns as the dissident Goldman-Morrow tendency which emerged in that same period; ultimately both Farrell and most members of that group shifted their allegiance completely to Shachtman's Workers party. Party affairs swirled around Farrell, although the inner life of the party was not his main concern; the inner life of the radical intellectual circles was much more so:

> That's why Farrell was not and should not have been a member of the party [Novack later said]. Unless one is convinced of the necessity of building a vanguard revolutionary party, one doesn't belong. That question becomes the ongoing center of personal and intellectual activities—it is the vantage point from which you view and see everything. Farrell wasn't situated in that central place.[43]

The political grouping in the Socialist Workers party led by Albert Goldman and Felix Morrow developed an opposition around questions of the assessment of the possibilities for postwar upsurges in Europe and the use of slogans in trade union work, and advocated an aggressive orientation toward unifying the Socialist Workers party with Shachtman's Workers party. Furthermore, the group made allegations against the Cannon leadership of the party, suggesting the existence of a cult or clique of followers and the use of unwarranted bureaucratic organizational methods. The grouping crystallized while Goldman, Morrow, and Cannon were all in jail, and the internal party struggle lasted until 1946.[44]

In the spring of 1944, Farrell submitted a lengthy letter for publication in the Socialist Workers party journal, *Fourth International*. He wrote to protest the contents of two of its previous articles: one was a description of Cannon on his way to prison, written by Joseph Hansen, which had been subjected to ridicule by Dwight Macdonald's *Politics* in May. Farrell agreed with Macdonald that the article was a "nauseous . . . mixture of sentimentality, smugness and leader-worship." The second article that Farrell protested was a critique of Max Shachtman's views by Harry Frankel (pseudonym for Harry Braverman). While Farrell did not agree with Shachtman's "bureaucratic collectivist" theory of the Soviet Union, he nevertheless felt that Frankel "substituted vituperation for argument and analysis." Farrell described a number of instances in which he believed methods "unworthy of Marxism" were used, and he concluded:

> I am, as is well known, not a member of your party. But I have collaborated with you on defense cases. I have expressed sympathy with you. On more than one occasion, I have made it clear to Max Shachtman and his collaborators that I did not agree with the theory of bureaucratic collectivism. The fact that I have done this causes me to feel all the more imperatively that it is my duty to send you this protest. Also: I admire the organized will which your party has shown. I admire your spirit of optimism and confidence. I admire the many examples of dedication to ideals and sacrifice for superpersonal loyalties which your party has displayed. But none of these virtues can, in any way, excuse the Frankel attack.

I am fearful that if articles such as these two [by Hansen and Frankel] continue to appear, their only effect will be that of working harm, not good. Gross sentimentality, unbending rigidity, unfair attacks on opponents—these are all dangerous. I hold them to be indefensible.[45]

The *Fourth International* refused to publish Farrell's letter; the editors believed that it was a means, or could be used as a means, of Farrell's interfering from the outside in the internal dispute between Cannon's followers and the Goldman-Morrow group. (The Goldman-Morrow group was also charging a cult atmosphere and excessive factionalism toward the Shachtman party.) The supporters of Goldman and Morrow protested this move as suppression, but the leaders of the Socialist Workers party restricted publication of Farrell's letter to their *Internal Discussion Bulletin* series. After waiting several months for the *Fourth International* to print his letter, Farrell released it to *Politics* and *New International,* where it appeared in December and November, 1944. (In *Politics,* Farrell prefaced the letter with a strong statement defending Leninism and criticizing Macdonald.)

The response of Cannon's majority group was blunt and to the point. The *Internal Bulletin* of April 1945 printed a statement from Cannon (written August 29, 1944) which declared the tone of Farrell's letter "rude and brutal," and "dishonest" in its representation of Frankel's article. A second statement, published in January 1945, after the appearance of Farrell's letter in the *New International* and *Politics,* was even more critical. The gist of Cannon's remarks, titled "An Insult to the Party" (referring to the demand of Goldman-Morrow supporters that Farrell's letter be publicly printed), stated that the party was comprised of professional revolutionaries who must work out their own problems; individuals like Farrell, "whose main interests and occupations lie in other fields," were unqualified to instruct the professionals. Cannon, in fact, lumped Farrell with Macdonald, "the archetype of these political Alices in Wonderland."

Cannon's statement was, within a short time, circulated among the anti-Stalinist left, and in July 1946 *Politics* published excerpts with Dwight Macdonald's commentary, charging Cannon and his party with constituting simply a variant of Stalinism:

> For years [Macdonald wrote] James T. Farrell has been a loyal and devoted fellow-traveler of the Trotskyists. Although personally I think he was *too* loyal, in the sense that he should have been more awake to the undemocratic ideology whose effects he has now himself experienced, one can only admire the moral courage with which he has stuck to his revolution-ary-socialist convictions while most other American intellectuals have been abandoning them. When the leaders of the Socialist Workers Party were persecuted in such a disgraceful fashion by the Department of Justice, Farrell not only lent his literary prestige to the defense committee, of which he was chairman, but also gave much time and work to it—speaking, writing pamphlets, carrying on correspondence. His letter to the *Fourth International* objecting to Hansen's article (and also to what he considered an unfair polemic against Max Shachtman in the same magazine) was obviously intended as a *friendly* criticism, not as a breaking off of political relations. Not only did the *Fourth International* refuse to print the letter, but now we see that the party boss [reference to Cannon] considers that Farrell has insulted the party by presuming to write it. Result: Farrell has now transferred his allegiance to the rival Shachtman group, the Workers Party.[46]

The next month, the *New International* (organ of Shachtman's Workers party) carried its own feature article on the Farrell-Cannon altercation, printing not only copies of Cannon's statements, but an answer to them by Albert Goldman (which had originally been published in a Socialist Workers party *Internal Bulletin*). Goldman described Farrell as a "devoted and courageous supporter of the Trotskyist movement" and an "educated Marxist" who had "studied and read as much Marxist theory as leading elements in the [Socialist Workers] Party." Therefore, Farrell's views on political matters should be welcome contributions, and

Goldman charged that it was a blatantly Stalinist notion that politics was the special province of party professionals.[47]

Farrell had resigned as Chairman of the Civil Rights Defense Committee between the time his original letter had been refused publication in *Fourth International* and it was printed in other journals. The October 12, 1945 resignation was sent to George Novack. Although Farrell agreed to remain a member of the CRDC itself, he explained that the Committee had been inactive since early in the winter of 1945, when the last of the Minneapolis defendants returned from prison. Farrell offered his collaboration in future cases.[48]

Farrell's correspondence with George Novack in the summer of 1945 indicates that their personal relations were still intact: Novack was supplying Farrell with periodicals and quotations from Marx, and Farrell was sending Novack his latest books. But some of the communications from Farrell were curt notes and contained references to the Cannon statements.[49] Nevertheless, a long letter to Novack (then in Boston) in February 1946 discussed the Maltz controversy and theoretical aspects of the Soviet Union's evolution since the purge trials.[50] (But that same month, a letter from Farrell to John Dewey—proposing a campaign to raise the question of the Moscow Trials in connection with the Nurenberg Trials to confirm that there was no complicity between the Nazis and Old Bolsheviks—spoke disparagingly of recent internal events in the Cannon party.) [51] In the spring of 1947, conflicts flared up again, and the correspondence between Farrell and Novack indicates that relations were close to being terminated. In letters of March 8 and March 10 addressed to Novack, but probably circulated among others, Farrell cited a list of grievances against Cannon and the Socialist Workers party.[52] In this period Farrell's literary contributions were appearing in Shachtman's rival *New International* almost as a regular feature.

In the spring of 1946, Farrell contributed to a *Politics* magazine discussion called "New Roads." He spoke on behalf of the revolutionary Marxist position. In an exchange with Macdonald, Farrell argued a defense of Leninism against the charge that it led logically to Stalinism; and he also echoed Trotsky's point that the tendency to hide behind abstract human values covered up a political retreat (which, in Farrell's view, had been happening each month in *Politics*). Macdonald defended his own numerous political changes, charging that they were preferable to Farrell's faith in a system.[53]

However, two years later, in April 1948, Farrell, along with Albert Goldman, announced what was effectively a break with the Shachtman group over the Marshall Plan. In a letter to their paper, *Labor Action*, Farrell stated his disagreement with the Workers party's opposition to the plan, emphasizing that the fight against Stalinism was the paramount concern, and that the capitalist reconstruction of Western Europe was better than no reconstruction: "Only American wealth and power stands in the way of Stalinist expansion." [54] In the following months, Farrell became Chairman of the Independent Voters for Norman Thomas, a body which included Daniel Bell, Van Wyck Brooks, Babette Deutsch, Irwin Edman, Erich Fromm, Sidney Hook, Harold Isaacs, C. Wright Mills, William Phillips, Philip Rahv, Meyer Schapiro, Edmund Wilson, and Bertram D. Wolfe.[55] In his call for Albert Einstein to back Thomas rather than Henry Wallace, Farrell proclaimed the Socialist party as the vehicle for building a "Third Force" between Stalinism and capitalism.[56]

Farrell's break with the Trotskyists was complete, and certainly bitter. In October he defended Norman Thomas against an attack by the campaign manager of the Socialist Workers party, George Clarke. Farrell claimed that Clarke, in a public statement, had made false innuendoes on Norman Thomas because the old Socialist was not in jail during World War II like the Trotskyist presidential candidate, Farrell Dobbs. (Farrell pointed out that both he and Norman Thomas had defended Dobbs against imprisonment.) Bringing up once more the offensive Hansen article on Cannon's trip to prison, Farrell ridiculed the Trotskyists' claim that they were "the only moral people." He also charged that the theory of the workers state was "political lunacy." "Monkeying around with this socialist splinter," Farrell warned, "will get you at least two handfuls of slivers." [57]

Farrell's published speech, *Truth and Myth About America*,[58] argued the view that Americans had become "the heirs of Western civilization" and that "only American wealth and power has protected freedom in the West of Europe." In mid-1950, Farrell addressed both the Cannon and Shachtman groups in the pages of the *New Leader,* ridiculing them for what Trotsky called "A failure of correspondence between the subjective and the objective." [59] History, to Farrell, had now become simply a plane of struggle between contending forces; there were no longer any Marxian "laws" of prognosis.[60]

7.

The Literary Record

I have attempted to create out of the life I have seen, known, experienced, heard about, and imagined, a panoramic story of our days and years, a story which would continue through as many books as I would be able to write.

James T. Farrell, 1973 [1]

The clearest manifestations of Trotsky's impact on Farrell were inspirational and political; but there was a special bond in their mutual search for "new perspectives" for Marxist writers and intellectuals. As a novelist, Farrell emerged from the 1920s looking favorably upon the literary tradition of modern realism and naturalism; but as an intellectual, with a wide-ranging knowledge of history and philosophy, he condemned the limited vistas of Dreiser, Anderson, and others. Originally, Farrell advanced beyond these other writers in his assimilation of the pragmatic social philosophy and psychology of Dewey and Mead. Like the New York intellectuals around *Partisan Review*, Farrell believed in the necessity of literary as well as Marxist tradition; and unlike

132

Max Eastman, and many in the Stalinist school of the early 1930s, Farrell accepted the 1920s revolution in technique and sensibility (although he found it inadequate for the 1930s).

Drawn initially to ideals he mistakenly associated with the Stalinist movement, Farrell felt a visceral disgust with the Communists' literary politics and began to forge a critique. Gradually, as in the case of other theoretically oriented intellectuals of an independent mind and revolutionary outlook, he came to prefer the critique that Trotsky had evolved of Stalinist policy: It provided greater depth, breadth, and the authenticity of being espoused by a genuine revolutionary leader.

We have examined in detail how Trotsky influenced the course of Farrell's intellectual development and his literary criticism. Although this study was predicated on the assumption that prior scholarship has revealed the foundations of Farrell's novels in the realism-naturalism school, augmented by pragmatic philosophy and social psychology, previous chapters have already provided several demonstrations of the considerable influence of Trotsky even on Farrell's fiction (manifest in a subordinate and complementary way).

It has been affirmed that Farrell's world of fictional creation in the 1930s and 1940s was imaginatively created primarily from the experiences of his childhood—especially from his observation of the social forces involved in the fall of Studs Lonigan types, as well as from his comprehension of the ordeal requisite for escape from the cultural shackles which victimized the O'Neill and O'Flaherty (Farrell and Daly) families. Farrell was brooding over and formulating the underlying concepts of his first two major cycles of novels in the late 1920s. Had Farrell succumbed, like so many other young plebeian writers, to the pressures of Stalinism or commercialism during the early 1930s, it is doubtful that either the Studs Lonigan trilogy would have been completed, or the O'Neill-O'Flaherty series ever written; for, as has been shown, these works were undertaken in defiance of the Stalinist line, government and local censors, and popular taste. Although Farrell's central literary projects were grounded in the 1920s, it is justifiable to assert that his gravitation toward Trotskyism was one important aid which assisted him in standing fast against currents which could have undermined the realization of his goals in fiction during the thirties and forties.

Trotskyism gave Farrell, the author of fiction, a revolutionary perspective for the sustenance of his art. The qualities Farrell came to admire the most in Trotsky—his faith in his ideas, his willingness to stand alone in defiance of Stalinism and capitalism—were those which nourished Farrell in his own struggles. Farrell's fight to keep art free from various forms of dictatorial and commercial corruption was as firm as Trotsky's resolution to liberate the revolutionary workers' movement from Stalinism. Farrell's search for truth in the Moscow Trials, and his willingness to face it, stemmed from the same urge which drove him to ruthlessly probe the world of Danny O'Neill.

But in addition to this general impact of Trotsky on the course of Farrell's fiction, it would be hard to imagine that Farrell's intense involvement with Trotsky (the man and his ideas), his impassioned defense of Trotsky, his thorough reading and re-reading of Trotsky's major works, his immersion in the milieu of Trotskyist and left-wing anti-Stalinists; his political battles against the Popular Front from a Trotskyist perspective, his adherence to the Trotskyist conception of the struggle against fascism—that all this could have passed without some specific observable impact on Farrell's fiction. And, of course, the evidence is there.

If one surveys the large quantity of Farrell's fiction which concerns radical intellectuals and particularly the Stalinist movement, there is one overriding characteristic: the conception of Stalinism, with its cultural arm, as a deforming and perfidious social movement. V. F. Calverton noted the absence of this approach in *A Note on Literary Criticism;* Farrell's polemic, Calverton had argued, seemed to be mainly against the ignorance of various Communist party critics. However, if the Trotskyist notion of Stalinism remained undiscussed in *A Note on Literary Criticism* for tactical reasons, the situation was soon reversed. In the following months and years Farrell demonstrated no lack of aggressiveness in promoting a Trotskyist understanding of political and cultural Stalinism in its Third Period, Popular Front, wartime, and post-Browder phases. (It was precisely this kind of incisive political critique which made Farrell anathema to the Stalinists and to those liberals who chose to ally with them.) And to some degree, Trotskyist critiques of the phases of Stalinism are concepts underlying parts of two novels (*The Road Between* and *Yet Other Waters*), scores of short stories, and one important play, "The Mowbray Family."

Farrell's fictional world of the Stalinist political-cultural movement is not peopled with simple scoundrels, conspirators, or especially naive or warped individuals (although some of these types are present). As a social force, Stalinism is portrayed as a magnet of attraction, offering (in its different periods) combinations of material and spiritual rewards. In the beginning of *Yet Other Waters* (depicting Stalinism in transition from the Third Period to the Popular Front), novelist Bernard Carr and Mel Morris (the editor of *Social Theatre*) have a revealing discussion. Mel, to whom the party has given a magazine and an audience, sings praises to what the Stalinists have done for him in a very material sense:

> "Look how we've both got ahead already," Mel went on. "We're going places. And the Movement's going places. After the Writers Congress next month, Bernie, there's going to be nothing to stop us in American culture. You remember how we both came to New York a few years ago, poor and unknown, without a pot to piss in?" [2]

The pull and appeal of the Communist movement is described in other Farrell stories, such as "John Hitchcock," which treats a starving book reviewer attracted as well as repelled by the movement:

> Many writers ... had gone left. In the circles in which he moved, Marxism, Revolution, the Communist Party, were constant subjects of loud discussion. ... Few of those who participated in these discussions were well read in Marxism; few knew the history of the Russian Revolution; and the level of the discussions was generally rigid, sloganistic. The Communists and fellow travelers who defended the Party line consistently spoke with great confidence and self-assurance, with, literally, the conceit of history in their voices. ... Most of

them were in circumstances essentially similar to those in which John found himself. They were declassed intellectuals. They wanted to be writers, critics, employees in publishing houses, figures in the literary life of New York. Times were bad, very bad in the publishing business. America was in the depths of the Hoover era. There was widespread unemployment. There were riots, starvation, hunger marches. American economy was shaken. The future looked miserable. The declassed intellectuals were insecure, shaky, worried. They did not know where to turn. The effort to survive harried them, warped their character. Communists and fellow travelers spoke to them with assurance and self-confidence, convinced that they were absolutely right.[3]

Fear and insecurity made them more susceptible to the pull; there was also idealism—the kind of idealism which moved Bernard Carr during the 1927 Sacco-Vanzetti demonstration (and which he tended to associate with the Communists). As Farrell later wrote: "Stalinism was . . . a house of cultural assignation, where one guy could get two girls for the night, the glamour girl of success, and poor little Nell, the beautiful but ragged proletarian girl of integrity." [4] Yet, as Farrell's stories reveal—and as the record authenticates—for most of the plebeian writers the success was short-lived. Many pro-Stalinists (such as Henry Roth, Robert Cantwell, Jack Conroy, Clara Weatherwax, Leane Zugsmith, Edwin Seaver, Isadore Schneider, Mike Gold, Edwin Rolfe, and Edward Newhouse) ended up writing little fiction, and much of that was soon forgotten. And, like many other characters in Farrell's stories, his literary representations of these pro-Stalinist writers end up as middle-aged men with lost dreams.[5]

Intellectuals who gravitated toward the Trotskyists tended to write fiction about themselves, their group and its problems, frequently in the form of *romans à clef*. Max Eastman's *Venture,* Edmund Wilson's *I Thought of Daisy,* Tess Slesinger's *The Unpossessed,* Mary McCarthy's *The Oasis,* are a few examples. And Farrell is no exception to the trend, especially inasmuch as *The Road Between* and *Yet Other Waters* are peopled with an abundance of figures from the radical literary movement. Some of these characters operate in other fiction as well, with the same or similar names. The degree of the portrait's accuracy seems to fall into one of three categories: the recreation of a person in full detail; the creation of characters who simply make statements or perform acts once carried out by an actual person; the depiction of composite or hybrid figures.

Jake (a recurring figure in several stories) is extremely suggestive of Joseph Freeman, especially in his attempts to hold dissident fellow travelers together by criticizing the Communist party's sectarianism in private. (In fact, like the Freeman observed in Farrell's diary, Jake even praises Trotsky in secret.) Certainly the short story "The Dialectic," which embodies a Trotskyist critique of the affinity of liberalism and Stalinism in the late 1930s, features a character very much like Joe Freeman. The story tells of two young students who became radicalized in the early 1930s. Jake is an admirer of Trotsky and Eddie seeks to emulate John Reed. Jake, however, joins the Communist party and a decade later is forced to suppress his real views in regard to Trotsky and the Moscow Trials (as was Freeman).[6] Eddie, in contrast, goes to Moscow as a correspondent, becomes disillusioned, returns to the United States, and is treated as an outcast by the Stalinists. But in a dialectical reversal at the end of the story, Jake is expelled by the Communists and Eddie becomes one of their allies in the Popular Front.[7]

In Farrell's fictional world, Jake and Mark Singer (a character resembling Mike Gold) are older cultural leaders of the Communist party, who kept the movement going in the 1920s. Other likely fictional representations of real persons are: Sherman Scott, literary editor of the *New Freedom* (Malcolm Cowley, literary editor of the *New Republic*); Pat Delvin (Jack Conroy); Moses Kallisch (Isador Schneider); Percival Longacre (Archibald MacLeish); Paul Drummond (John Howard Lawson); Sam Steckler (Max Lieber, a literary agent later alleged to have GPU ties); Mel Morris (Herb Kline); Ellison (Earl Browder); Harry Oliver (John Chamberlain); Keefe (Kenneth Burke); Larry Watkins (Clarence Hathaway); Lester Owens (James Rorty); Sigmund Eisenberg (Alexander Trachtenberg; Frank Darlen (Edward Dahlberg); George Somovitch (Moissaye Olgin); Lloyd Street (Whittaker Chambers).[8]

The Bernard Carr trilogy, although it relies heavily on Farrell's personal experiences, was intended to portray the process of the political and moral corruption of writers in the 1930s. Carr was to become the half-willing prey of Stalinism at first, and then probably fall victim to commercial corruption. Obviously the original plan never materialized. And if one studies the Carr trilogy seeking an autobiographical representation of Farrell's experiences in the thirties, the books are especially disconcerting because they compress nearly fifteen subsequent years into the story. Thus Carr's break with the Stalinists in *Yet Other Waters* becomes a separation from the revolutionary movement per se. As one commentator noted, *Yet Other Waters* is not at all the kind of book Farrell would have written in the thirties or early forties. It has the distinct flavor of Farrell's views of the very late forties and after.[9]

For example, in *Yet Other Waters* the Trotskyists are presented essentially as a wing of the Stalinist movement—an opinion Farrell came to hold during those later years in direct contradiction to his earlier views. This portrayal is accomplished through the character of Lester Owens (suggestive of James Rorty), the anarchist poet who once served on the editorial board of *Mass Action*. In *Yet Other Waters*, Owens organizes an Open Letter of Protest against the Stalinists' disruption of a Socialist party meeting. Owens explains to Carr that although Leon Trotsky was a great man, his followers are about as bad as the Stalinists. He describes how the Trotskyists broke up a Non-Partisan Labor Committee because they (the Trotskyists) were planning to amalgamate with another group. The period of brief collaboration with the Trotskyists, for Owens, was simply a "second merry-go-round." Consequently, when Carr draws back from the Stalinists, he is left only with some vague literary projects and his shaky relationship with his wife as alternatives to politics. Although it concerns the 1930s, *Yet Other Waters* is in viewpoint a novel of the late forties and early fifties, and can be fully assessed only in the context of Farrell's political and personal life in those years. Nevertheless, this *roman à clef* about the tribulations of literary intellectuals is in the genre which seems most typical of novelists in the radical anti-Stalinist current.

"The Martyr" is more authentically a story of its time (the mid-forties). It demonstrates the profound emptiness of the lives of the men from the Communist literary milieu. A fictionalized account of the famous post-Browder literary dispute in the Communist party, it tells of Leonard Luckman, a thinly disguised Albert Maltz, who returns to New York after six years in Hollywood. At age forty, he makes an ill-fated attempt to change the literary policy of the Communist party that he once helped forge but now feels has sterilized his literary work. With keen psychological insight, Farrell probes the convoluted logic of self-deception by which the characters justify their own self-betrayals.

It was frequently because of their approach to character development that Farrell judged novels of the pro-Stalinist writers to be shallow; no doubt Farrell felt drawn to and was influenced by Trotsky on a literary plane because of the marvelous character portraits contained in *The History of the Russian Revolution*. Of these, Farrell once wrote:

> He [Trotsky] saw in everyone the representative of a class or of a social group, and in everyone's ideas he perceived their political consequences. His estimates of character, despite the charges of his critics, were generally not personal: they were political and intellectual. His brilliant character vignettes in *The History of the Russian Revolution* are actually social studies in miniature.[10]

Although the class differences of characters—for example, in the O'Neill-O'Flaherty books, Jim O'Neill, the worker, and Al O'Flaherty, the salesman—were in the material itself, Trotsky's approach may have helped Farrell make full use of all possibilities. The crowning achievement was probably Farrell's magnificent portrait of his father, represented by Jim O'Neill, as the embodiment of the American working man in *Father and Son*.[11]

Additionally, since Farrell was a novelist of character, the nature of the Communist movement was also revealed in Farrell's fiction by the way it attracted and shaped character. Some of Farrell's best literary portraits feature this concern: especially that of Norman Griel in "Victim or Hero?", a careful representation of a journalist (again, suggestive of a real figure) pulled into the

Stalinist movement. Griel suppresses his doubts about the Moscow Trials and tries to escape his deteriorating personal life through a trip to Spain (during the Civil War). There he is accidentally killed, having been propelled into the situation by a destiny almost (but not totally) beyond his control.[12]

"Breakfast" is a character sketch of Arthur Stein, who sneers at bourgeois culture and clings to a notion of Marxism as the "locomotive of history." [13] "A Story About Money" is another portrayal, although cruder, of a wealthy cultural dilettante who ends up in the Communist party.

Other stories tend to reflect concerns of those in the anti-Communist left. "Comrade Stanley" focusses on the intrigue and factional mentality of the Communist movement. "A Love Story of Our Time," similar to Dos Passos's *Adventures of a Young Man,* exhibits a young anticapitalist poet literally seduced into going to Spain, only to discover the true treacherous role of the Stalinists there and be denounced.

Farrell's attitude after the forties toward the Trotskyist movement—a hostile one in most of his published fiction—is concentrated in a group of five stories (in addition to the appearance of Joseph Benton in "Tom Carroll"). Some of this work consists of character likenesses: for example, "The Mayor's Committee," in which the clever, witty, and somewhat shallow narrator suggests Max Shachtman, and "Episodes of a Return," in which Albert Goldman may have been the model for the tired ex-radical and former Smith Act victim. "Digging Our Graves" is a bitter satire about the impotence of a squabbling, sectarian left, with swipes at James Cannon (probably suggested by the figure described as "the Lenin of America if he hadn't drunk whiskey") and Dwight Macdonald (the likely point of reference in "The Yale man's moral resolution").[14]

The most extensive fictional critique of the Trotskyist movement is "The Renegade." [15] It is the story of Hal, an arrogant unattractive person who breaks with the Communists almost accidentally and gravitates toward Trotskyism. There he is taken under the wing of the party's philosopher (reputed to be a budding David Ryazanov), Joseph Zinn, whose party name is "Benton." (This is the same name as that of the character resembling George

Novack in "Tom Carroll," and is also meant to be a fictional portrait of Farrell's one-time friend. Patrick Nolan suggests James Cannon, and certain of Hal's experiences may have been inspired by Felix Morrow, although Hal seems much more of a composite figure than the other two.) Hal is impressed by the Trotskyists' righteous talk about the integrity of their party, and their claim to be "the only moral people."

Under the supervision of Benton—a man perpetually on the alert for potentially dangerous scratches and infections which can lead to political gangrene—Hal rises to the position of a party journalist. He quits college and joins the small group of dull, unimaginative, but courageous and hard-working members. However, at the end of the story, again almost accidentally, Hal discovers himself to be a leading member of an opposition group and, although he re-cants, he is expelled by Benton. "The Renegade" is a hostile lit-erary reaction against the factional struggles of the Trotskyist movement, which had irked Farrell at least since the time of the imbroglio in the Socialist party. But the unkind portraits of Novack and Cannon introduce an element of subjective personal bitterness that is rare even in Farrell's most autobiographical fiction, and is an index of the deep wound left by his disillusion-ment with the Trotskyist movement.

With the exception of *Tommy Gallagher's Crusade,* the collection *When Boy-Hood Dreams Come True* (1946) is probably the book of fiction most overtly reflective of Farrell's positive attitude toward the Trotskyists before his break with them. This is especially evidenced in the play contained in the book, "The Mowbray Family." Here, in contrast to *Yet Other Waters,* we have anti-Stalinism combined with a radical alternative. In this three-act comedy (written with Hortense Farrell), the wealthy home of the Mowbrays has become filled with a gallery of Stalinists from the Popular Front movement, because of the foolish gullibility of Mrs. Mowbray. The play contains excellent social-political likenesses of all the types attracted to the Stalinist-liberal enterprise: Mortimer, the Lost Generation poet of patrician character who is revered because he, for one, is now "doing" something besides just "talking"; Sandy Warren, a hardboiled Communist party journal-ist; Eric, a tortured middle-class writer.

However, counterposed to this morass is Philip Bentley, a disciple of John Dewey and a philosophy instructor, who is anticapitalist, revolutionary, but opposed to the totalitarian features of Stalinism and who predicts the Hitler-Stalin Pact. (The Pact occurs at the climax of the play when it is announced over the radio.) Philip seems a positive force, and he is clearly a Trotskyist intellectual, although not an orthodox Marxist (Farrell, in fact, makes Philip a conscious opponent of dialectical materialist philosophy, and attributes to the Stalinist, Mortimer, a speech on dialectics similar to Trotsky's brief treatment in "The ABC of Dialectical Materialism.") [16]

Farrell's short fiction is also permeated with representations of other social types cast up by the radical movement, including the exiled left-wing Social Democrat from Spain in "Man on an island of History"; the narrow politico, "Dumbrovic"; the ex-Stalinists in "The Lady and the Masters of History"; the former labor radicals in "Reunion Abroad." The most explicitly revolutionary of all Farrell's short works is "Summer Morning in Dublin." This is reportage of the first order, in the 1930s genre, and ends with a revolutionary summons (after a survey of Dublin's brutal poverty): ". . . the only alternative is for all workers to rise up and seize power themselves." [17]

Especially when Farrell is compared to other American realists like Dreiser, his work shows indications of an international and historical consciousness which Trotsky's Marxism may have partially inspired and partially broadened. In a taped interview with David Madden, Farrell emphasized the importance of the first World War at the beginning of the second volume of the Studs Lonigan books, an event which resulted in an "unsure moral consciousness" after its occurrence.[18] Apparently an important conception underlying Farrell's forthcoming book *How Our Day Began* (of which some excerpts have been published), is the world-shaking opening of what Lenin deemed "the imperialist epoch" of war and revolution, in 1914:

> We were born the same year and, thus, we can say that we are of the same generation and have felt some of the same general pressures of history on our own lives. Our characters, our

minds, our feelings, have grown, developed, evolved within the field where these pressures are at work. You are Dutch and Jewish and were born in Amsterdam, and I am American and Irish, and was born in Chicago. We are children of the twentieth century, but we were born before the twentieth century became fully what it is. In 1914, this century exploded in its own face, and ever since it has been face-lifting and doctoring itself, and seeking to develop a better mirror in order that it may see its own reflected image more clearly.[19]

Nevertheless, it is not the argument of this book that Farrell's outlook derives from a single source of influence—be it a man like Trotsky, a historic movement like socialism, or a liberal philosophy like pragmatism. Rather, what has been demonstrated is how Farrell's social, moral, and political concerns not only underlie much of his fiction but also how they are expressed in his fiction—sometimes more directly than at other times. A comprehensive and judicious assessment of Farrell's contributions to American letters is thus impossible without taking into account his long and intense involvement with Marxism and Trotskyism. If Farrell's work had been exclusively provincial rather than intertwined with political events of the day (even, in some instances, virtually rotating around international events), then one might be justified in ignoring the relationship between Farrell's literary output and his involvement with Trotsky and revolutionary Marxism. But Farrell's work is not provincial—nor divorced from his Marxist experience.

8.

Conclusion

Two currents of political literati received special attention in the 1960s and 1970s. The first includes those attracted by the Russian Revolution and the Soviet state between 1917 and 1939. The second is the grouping—most notably Ezra Pound, T.S. Eliot, D.H. Lawrence, and W.B. Yeats—whose semi-fascist leanings are documented in John R. Harrison's *The Reactionaries: A Study of the Anti-Democratic Intelligentsia* (1966).[1] The apparent political excesses, contradictions, and turnabouts of these and more recent twentieth-century authors provoked Alfred Kazin into a 1973 diatribe called "The Writer as Political Crazy."[2]

No doubt the radical left has had its share of dilettantes, egomaniacs, and apolitical innocents blown hither and yon by the storms of wars, revolutions, and the Great Depression. To decry various authors as "crazy" in political views, however, can obscure the fact that as a group politicized writers articulated opinions of important layers of the intellectual stratum of the middle class. Furthermore, such an approach underplays the ultimate source of the madness of the times: social and political systems in economic chaos, competition, upheaval, and decay.

A more useful characterization might be one emphasizing the hybrid outlook of most American left-wing writers. In comparison with the theoretical consistency of European revolutionary intellectuals—such as V. I. Lenin, Leon Trotsky, and Rosa Luxemburg—American socialist writers seem a congeries of contradictions. Among novelists, one thinks of Jack London's belief in Nordic supremacy; Upton Sinclair's Puritanism and faddism; Theodore Dreiser's embracing both the Communist party and religion in the last year of his life. In the crisis of the 1930s, many Amrican left-wing writers combined a cacophony of utopian moral visions, Enlightenment faith in reason, and pragmatic political responses; the involvement of most in working-class political movements was superficial and episodic.[3]

Although not totally free from hybrid qualities, the record of James T. Farrell shows important differences. Farrell's seriousness about the study of philosophy, history, and politics motivated Murray Kempton to write in *Part of Our Time* that "There were many ways in which he [Farrell] was the best educated young writer of his time." [4] Farrell's commitment to political activism has been an integral component of his literary and intellectual life. "I don't know of another novelist, American or European, whose writings have been so occupied with day to day politics over so long a period," recalled Meyer Schapiro.[5]

This study provides evidence that James T. Farrell was the most prolific and successful American novelist in the thirties who adhered to revolutionary politics (if a "revolutionary" is considered someone who advocates the overthrow of the existing social system). The influence of revolutionary ideas, especially those of Trotsky, was apparent mainly in his critical and polemical writing, and to a lesser extent in his fiction. But it was largely due to his agreement with the way Trotsky interpreted Marxist doctrine in the sphere of literature and art that Farrell was able successfully to combine intensive and productive literary, critical and polemical work throughout the thirties and forties.

Trotsky's interpretation urged writers and artists to come forward and campaign for working-class emancipation and social revolution; it also clearly differentiated between these responsibilities and the artistic project, which demanded, above all, that the writer be faithful to his or her vision and renounce dictates from any party, government or authority. Many pro-Stalinist writers either ceased to produce or, as in the case of Richard Wright, were forced to abandon the Marxist movement altogether. But Farrell was able to intensify his socialist involvement while working productively on his main fictional task in those years: the O'Neill-O'Flaherty series. This work was political only by implication; its object was the depiction of human character and the forces shaping it, expressed in the realist-naturalist literary mode:

> As a matter of fact [Farrell wrote], I do not hesitate to state that one of the fundamental purposes of practically all my fiction is that of recreating a sense of the American way of life, recreating it concretely in terms of the careers and patterns of destiny of many who have lived and are living in certain social environments in certain sections of this country.

That is not to say that Farrell, like Max Eastman, advocated a total separation between art and politics; on the contrary, Farrell acknowledged that Marxian concepts were employed quite consciously in his fiction:

> The very structure of these novels [A *World I Never Made* and *No Star Is Lost*] is based on the hypothesis that there is a class structure to society. The author looks on character, personality, the *self* as a social product. The *self* is developed in society. The nature of the self is delimited by society. To make such statements does not deny individuality: rather, it seeks an hypothesis to explain individuality.[6]

Thus Farrell's approach was in harmony with Trotsky's view that writers should assimilate Marxist ideas as a framework for understanding society, but that they should still create artistic content that is consistent with the truth of their personal vision. Farrell, of course, took Trotsky's plea for artistic "truth" and welded it to the literary tradition of realism and naturalism, which he saw as primarily a struggle to express that "truth."

Additionally, in considering Trotsky's impact, it should be

recognized that much of Trotsky's writing on questions of literature was uneven and occasional: It was produced in response to
specific controversies or what he believed to be erroneous theories
or practices. Thus there are certain areas where the question of
Trotsky's influence on Farrell simply could not be relevant: for
example, in the area of technique and method (apart from the fact
that Trotsky maintained an openness to all approaches, while
writers under Stalinist influence tended to maintain a hostile
stance toward the literary experiments of the 1920s). It might be
argued that Farrell's greatest weakness as a writer was that he
failed to develop either sufficient consciousness about or a sophisticated theory of the uses of language in writing fiction, beyond
admirable but rather simple notions that language must serve the
end of accurately recreating character and environment. Marxist
aesthetics in general, including Trotsky's contribution, probably
did nothing to inspire Farrell in this regard, and if anything,
permitted a laxness. But there is also the question of human
capacity. It is a matter of record that writers of fiction on the left
have tended to be preoccupied mainly with content, and especially
with the recreation of social forces in literature. However, writers
who have placed the major emphasis on formal and linguistic
questions have been inclined toward apolitical or conservative
views. Thus it is not surprising that as *Partisan Review* abandoned
its revolutionary political thrust during the 1940s, its preoccupation with modernism and formalism intensified.

*   *   *

The unique features that combined to create the intellect and
literary achievement of James T. Farrell do not override the
conclusion that his evolution and development were paradigmatic
of the group of Trotskyist intellectuals. It is true that Farrell came
onto the New York literary scene in his own way, and that he
aggressively resisted the historic forces which disillusioned most of
his contemporaries and derailed them from the revolutionary
course several years earlier. Yet, as was noted in Chapter 1, there
existed decisive intellectual and political similarities between
Farrell and the group. These involved the nature of his intellectual

origins in the 1920s and his attitude toward Trotsky in the 1930s. The interaction of these qualities can be summarized by stating that within Farrell and most of the others of the group, there existed an intellectual conflict between the liberal pragmatist ideas they had assimilated in the 1920s and the revolutionary political conclusions which seemed to be demanded by the Depression and events of the 1930s. Their very important intellectual experiences in the 1920s, which gave them the critical-mindedness to withstand the pull of the Communist movement, also served to prevent their full acceptance of the Trotskyist program. Even Farrell, who embraced the political perspective of this program to a greater degree than most others in the group, still remained a pragmatist thinker in the Dewey-Mead tradition. From first to last he never fully embraced Marxist philosophy.

The liberal Progressivism of the twenties (with which pragmatism was identified) and the revolutionary Marxism of the thirties became symbolized, for most of the group, by the figures of John Dewey and Leon Trotsky. Philosophically, Hook, Farrell, and others aspired to reconcile Deweyism and Marxism in some fashion. Certainly the high point of the group's cohesiveness and political impact came during the campaign against the Moscow Trials, which brought Dewey and Trotsky together in reality, if only for a brief moment.

But the alliance between liberal pragmatism, an outlook ultimately rooted in the bourgeois-democratic revolution, and revolutionary Marxism, emanating most strongly from the Russian Revolution, did not endure. In the end it was largely through reevaluations of the Russian Revolution that the group called into question the revolutionary project. For some, the reassessment was sparked by disillusionment over the Moscow Trials; for others, it came following the Soviet invasions of Poland and Finland; for Farrell, it was primarily caused by concern over postwar Soviet expansionism.

Notes

Books and dissertations cited in the footnotes will be designated only by the author's last name and title; and in the case of books by James T. Farrell, only the title will be given. Fuller information will be found in the bibliography, where articles consulted but not referred to in the text are also listed.

Letters addressed to Wald are in the author's possession; all other correspondence, unpublished manuscripts, and James T. Farrell's unpublished diary for the 1930s (designated as "diary" in the footnotes) are in the Farrell Collection at the University of Pennsylvania. In referring to correspondence, James T. Farrell's name has been abbreviated to JTF.

Introduction: The Complementary Side of Farrell

1. *Nation*, 142 (June 24, 1936), 101.
2. Farrell prefers to call the five novels depicting the youth of Danny O'Neill the "O'Neill-O'Flaherty series." This includes *The Face of Time*, published ten years after *My Days of Anger*, which had previously appeared to be the concluding volume.

The name "Bernard Clare" was changed to "Bernard Carr" in the second novel of Farrell's third series of books, after a libel suit by a man who coincidentally happened to be named "Bernard Clare." The character will be referred to by the changed name, "Carr," in all three novels.

3. Six doctoral dissertations which treat Farrell as the major topic are listed in the bibliography, along with Edgar Branch's short book. Articles and essays on Farrell—some of which comprise major portions of some well-known books—are far too numerous to list in their entirety. But only one of these studies, Sanders' dissertation called *Pattern of Rejection*, contains anything approximating a substantial examination of Farrell's left-wing accomplishments. Sanders is generally accurate, although somewhat superficial due to brevity and the fact that Sanders restricts himself to the examination of a very limited amount of material.

Recent trends in literary criticism of Farrell are represented in a special Farrell issue of *Twentieth Century Literature*, 22 (February, 1976), which contains eight essays about different aspects of his work and an interview.

4. It should be pointed out, however, that Joseph Freeman was hardly comfortable in his role as a Stalinist cultural pace-setter. Felix Morrow, who was a friend of Freeman during 1930-33, wrote in an August 12, 1974 letter to Wald: "He [Freeman] was managing editor of the *New Masses* in those years but could hardly be gotten out of bed each day; he was in the grip of the [Communist] party but torn within by what he knew and by what he wanted to be—a poet. Specifically, he was in the grip of [Alexander] Trachtenberg, who was boss of all cultural matters. His fear of Trachtenberg was boundless."

5. Kempton, *Part of Our Time*, p. 131.

6. Cowley, *Think Back On Us: The Social Record*, p. 56. See also Aaron, *Writers on the Left*, pp. 75-76. For Alfred Kazin's opinions about the sources of Cowley's "sophisticated literary Stalinism," see Kazin, *Starting Out in the Thirties*, pp. 15-20.

7. Books that Farrell studied in the late 1920s and early 1930s included *Ethics*, in collaboration with James H. Tufts (1908); *How We Think* (1910); *Human Nature and Conduct* (1922); *Experience and Nature* (1925); *The Public and Its Problems* (1927); *The Quest for Certainty* (1929); *Individualism, Old and New* (1930). Further information about Dewey's impact on Farrell can be found in Lamont, *Dialogue on John Dewey*, passim.

8. Novack to Wald, April 29, 1973.

Chapter 1: Emergence from the Twenties

1. *New Freeman,* 1 (July 2, 1930), 374.
2. Cited in Kempton, *Part of Our Time,* p. 148. Kempton claims that Farrell made this remark to Whittaker Chambers during an argument in the *New Masses* offices in 1932 about the Communist slogan "Art is a Weapon."
3. *When Time Was Born,* pp. 13-14.
4. For Carmon's reminiscences of his role on the *New Masses,* written after a visit to the USSR, see *New Masses,* 21 (November 24, 1936), 13. James Henle of Vanguard Press was himself an old-time radical. Among other things, he had interviewed Leon Trotsky during Trotsky's brief stay in New York City just prior to the February 1917 revolution in Russia.
5. Interview with Farrell, November, 1973.
6. "I needed a work that would carry and predicate a vast series," JTF to Branch, July 2, 1969. This is quoted in Branch, *James T. Farrell,* p. 142.
7. *Boarding House Blues,* pp. 210-211.
8. *The Silence of History,* p. 7.
9. Ibid., p. 175.
10. The facts are in "The World I Grew Up In," *Commonweal,* 83 (February 25, 1966), 606-611.
11. *The Silence of History,* p. 132.
12. Ibid., p. 160.
13. The character George Raymond is suggestive of Farrell's friend Paul Caron; the same figure is called "Ed Lanson" in *Boarding House Blues* and *Ellen Rogers.*
14. The character who appears under the names "John Mason" and "Bill Baily" in Farrell's novels is based upon a real acquaintance of Farrell.
15. *My Days of Anger,* pp. 108-114.
16. *Bernard Clare,* pp. 82-94.
17. *Boarding House Blues,* p. 143.
18. Ibid., p. 141.
19. Ibid., p. 136.
20. Ibid., p. 150.
21. Ibid., p. 141.
22. Farrell makes this comment about the 1930 article in *The League of Frightened Philistines,* p. xii, where the piece is reprinted on pp. 149-153.
23. The preceding quotes are all from "Thirty and Under" in *The League of Frightened Philistines,* pp. 149-153. Farrell is in error when he refers to Irving Babbitt as "Dr."

24. *Saturday Review of Literature*, 6 (July 12, 1930), 1194.
25. *The Silence of History*, pp. 182-183.
26. *The Collected Poems of James T. Farrell*, p. 22.
27. *New York Sun* (October 15, 1932), 19.
28. *Saturday Review of Literature*, 7 (June 6, 1931), 879.
29. See Branch, *James T. Farrell*, pp. 24-28, for more details.
30. Interview with Farrell, November 1973.
31. Neagoe, *Americans Abroad*, p. 142.

Chapter 2: For New Perspectives

1. JTF to Patchen, May 10, 1937.
2. Aaron, *Writers on the Left*, pp. 300-303; Hicks, *Part of the Truth*, p. 130. Also, in Lewis Fried's doctoral dissertation ("The Naturalism of James T. Farrell") it is suggested that Farrell may have exaggerated or misunderstood the animosity welling up against him from pro-Stalinist circles (see pp. 146-148).
3. *New Masses*, 6 (December, 1930), 18. On page 22 Farrell is described simply as a Chicago "contributor to the magazines."
4. "The Scoop," *Daily Worker* (January 30, 1934), 5; "Studs Lonigan," *Partisan Review*, 1 (February-March 1934), 16-23; "Children of the Twilight," *New Masses*, 11 (May 29, 1934), 13-16.
5. *New Masses*, 12 (July 3, 1934), 28-29.
6. "In Reply to the Author," ibid., 32.
7. "Farrell's Progress," *New Masses*, 8 (July 1933), 29.
8. "Farrell Between Books," *New Masses*, 13 (October 30, 1934), 21-22.
9. *New Masses*, 15 (May 25, 1935), 25-26. Josephine Herbst's letters to Farrell prior to 1936 contain criticisms of the rigid literary outlooks of Gold and Tractenberg; they also attack Freeman for being too cowardly to stand up for his real opinions. Letters are in the Farrell Collection.
10. "Formula for a Best Seller," *New Masses*, 14 (March 19, 1935), 23-24; "Heavenly Visitation," *New Masses*, 15 (April 2, 1935), 32-33; "Another Washington Circus," *New Masses*, 16 (July 2, 1935), 33-34.
11. "A Connecticut Valley," *New Masses*, 16 (September 10, 1935), 28.
12. See the following issues of the *Daily Worker:* January 18, 1935, 5; April 30, 1935, 2; May 3, 1935, 2; August 6, 1935, 5; November 14, 1935, 1.
13. *New Republic*, 79 (June 27, 1934), 185.
14. *New Masses*, 14 (February 5, 1935), 7. See also JTF to Mary Farrell, February 17, 1935.
15. See the following letters: JTF to Mary Farrell, May 16, October 18, and November 2, 1932; JTF to Dorothy Farrell, August 28, 1933.

16. Dahlberg to JTF, July 17, 1933.
17. See the following letters: JTF to Mary Farrell, February 2, February 8, May 4, July 20, and October 24, 1934; JTF to Noah Fabricant, January 2, 1935; JTF to Mary Farrell, April 12, 1935.
18. JTF to Mary Farrell, April 22, 1935.
19. Hicks, *Part of the Truth*, p. 142.
20. All quotations are from *Partisan Review*, 2 (April-May 1935), 5-8.
21. JTF to Wald, February 5, 1974; and interview with Farrell, November 1973.
22. *Partisan Review and Anvil*, 3 (February 1936), 28-30.
23. Hart, *American Writers' Congress*, pp. 103-114. The speech reaffirmed Farrell's ongoing criticisms.
24. *Nation*, 137 (December 20, 1933), 714-715.
25. Farrell discussed the Conroy controversy at length in a letter to Branch, January 29, 1974.
26. *New Masses*, 10 (February 20, 1934), 24. Farrell's assessment of Dahlberg's *Those Who Perish* appeared under the title "In Search of the Image" in *New Masses*, 13 (December 4, 1934), 21-22, and was reprinted in *The League of Frightened Philistines*, pp. 154-160.
27. On February 7, 1934, Dahlberg wrote to Farrell that Granville Hicks was angered about his review in the *New Masses* and the remarks made about Farrell.
28. *New Masses*, 11 (April 24, 1934), 31.
29. JTF to Branch, January 29, 1974.
30. *New Letters*, 39 (Fall 1972), 49. In the dissertation by Fried, p. 142, it is claimed that Conroy had attacked Farrell in order to boost sales and have fun. Conroy denied this, however, in a letter to Wald, July 31, 1974.
31. Conroy to Wald, July 31, 1974. Farrell, however, denies that he ever labeled Conroy as "Cornrow" in a letter to Wald, August 10, 1974.
32. Conroy to Wald, July 31, 1974.
33. See the following issues of the *New Republic*: 142 (November 10, 1937), 22; 143 (December 1, 1937), 103-104; 143 (January 12, 1938), 286; 143 (February 16, 1938), 48. For further information on Ferguson, see Kazin's memoir in *Starting Out in the Thirties*, pp. 29-51. Conroy told his version of how the twenty-six names were obtained for the letter to the *New Republic* in *New Letters*, 39 (Fall 1972), 51.
34. Lovett to JTF, January 30, 1944.
35. *Carleton Miscellany*, 6 (Winter 1965), 38-39.
36. "Introduction," *Writers in Revolt*, p. xix. Conroy further explains that Nelson Algren ended up playing the role of Phyllis.
37. "Papa Anvil and Mother Partisan," *New Masses*, 18 (February 18, 1936), 22-23.
38. Numerous details are contained in Farrell's letter to Branch of

January 29, 1974, and in sections of Farrell's diary for the year 1936 (pp. 238, 239, 240, 247, 248). The original version of Josephine Herbst's letter is in the Farrell Collection.

39. _New Masses_, 13 (March 10, 1936), 20.
40. Ibid., 10.
41. _Nation_, 142 (March 4, 1936), 276-277; _Nation_, 142 (March 11, 1936), 314-315.
42. _American Spectator_, 4 (April 1936), 21-26.
43. "Theatre Chronicle," _Partisan Review and Anvil_, 3 (April 1936), 24.
44. JTF to Cantwell, February 4, 1936. The reference was probably to Granville Hicks.
45. JTF to Mary Farrell, March 3 and March 19, 1936.
46. JTF to Jack Farrell, May 28, 1936.
47. JTF to Nathan Adler, June 29, 1936.
48. _A Note on Literary Criticism_, p. 54.
49. Ibid., p. 186.
50. _New Masses_, 19 (June 23, 1936), 23-25.
51. _New Masses_, 20 (June 30, 1936), 23.
52. _New Masses_, 20 (July 14, 1936), 23.
53. _New Masses_, 20 (August 18, 1936), 23.
54. The Siegel letter and first letter by Schappes appear in ibid., 20 (August 18, 1936), 23. Farrell's answer to Schappes is in ibid., 20 (September 1, 1936), 22. Schappes' second letter is in ibid., 20 (September 22, 1936), 19.
55. _Nation_, 142 (June 24, 1936), 808-810.
56. Novack to JTF, July 3, 1936.
57. "Criticism at the Barricades," _Modern Monthly_, 10 (August 1936), 16-18, 31; "James T. Farrell and Leon Trotsky," _Modern Monthly_, 10 (October 1936), 15-17.
58. However, this is only a conjecture. In an August 12, 1974 letter to Wald, Felix Morrow commented that "I always found Calverton an honorable and selfless critic."
59. Interview with Farrell, November 1973. In his July 3, 1936 letter to Farrell, Novack wrote: "I was glad to see that Wilson gave Trotsky the credit you were obliged to withhold for tactical reasons."
60. Farrell was often at Yaddo between 1933 and 1935, according to his remarks in _Esquire_, 58 (December 1962), 275.
61. Interview with George Novack, October 28, 1972.

Chapter 3: James T. Farrell and George Novack in the 1930s

1. Interview with George Novack, November 1973.
2. This information was mentioned in a letter from Sidney Hook to

Lewis Corey, December 1, 1933. It is cited in Buhle, "Louis C. Fraina," p. 82.

3. A flavor of this project is conveyed in Novack's essay "U.S. Capitalism: National or International," *New International,* II (October 1935), 191-197.

4. A segment of the unpublished work is called *Civil War in New York,* and it concerns draft riots and labor movements of the period. Novack desired to build upon the work of Charles Beard and his conception of "The Second American Revolution," although he also regarded Beard's work as economic determinist and not dialectical materialist. A number of essays which resulted from this effort were recently collected in Novack, *America's Revolutionary Heritage.* However, many of Novack's other materials were lost in a fire at the Socialist Workers party's "Trotsky School" in the early 1950s.

5. Novack, *International Socialist Review,* 29 (March-April 1968), 28.

6. Novack to JTF, November 3, 1934. This was sent to Farrell at Yaddo.

7. "Chicago Childhood," unpublished manuscript in possession of George Novack.

8. Novack to JTF, undated. The contents suggest that it was written in late 1934 while Farrell was still at Yaddo.

9. ". . . I was prodigiously pleased to get an invitation to return to Yaddo. I had not for a moment expected that I would. Who do I have to thank for that welcome invitation?" Novack to JTF, April 5, 1935.

10. JTF to Ames, April 18, 1936.

11. Novack to JTF, July 3, 1936. Also, see the lengthy undated letter on events in Spain, which was probably written that same summer.

12. Diary, April 24, 1936, contains notes on the book.

13. Diary, July 3, 1936. Freeman remarked that Trotsky "is a wonderful writer."

14. Diary, July 26, 1936.

15. The book list is in the diary at the end of December 1936.

16. Diary, August 14, 1936.

17. Diary, September 18, 1936.

18. Diary, October 21, 1936.

19. Diary, December 31, 1936; January 6, 1937; and January 22, 1937. There are brief notations about arguments with Phillips and Rahv, who complained that the Trotskyists were incorrect and ineffective.

20. On June 3, 1936, Farrell noted in his diary that he had recently seen Edmund Wilson, and that Wilson made the following statement: "These last two years, Trotsky has been the conscience of the world." On September 5, 1936, Farrell noted in his diary that Harold Rosenberg praised the French Trotskyist paper *Lutte Ouvrière,* which

George Novack had sent. On July 26, 1936, Farrell recorded in his diary a conversation with Joseph Freeman in which the latter commented: "When the history of the Russian Revolution is written, Trotsky will have his rightful place."

21. A complete listing of Novack's *New International* articles published during the 1930s is contained in the *Combined Index to The New International, The Fourth International, and the International Socialist Review*, published by the Socialist Workers party.

22. Some of these lesser achievements are discussed in Chapter 7.

23. *Judith*, p. 286. This passage is reminiscent of some of the remarks made to Wald by Farrell in an interview, November 1973.

24. *Judith*, p. 309. The Hippodrome meeting is described by Lionel Abel in "New York: A Remembrance," *Dissent*, 8 (Summer 1961), 256. Abel was a sympathizer of the Trotskyists. His wife, Sherry, was the sister of Trotskyist lawyer Albert Goldman; later she was associated with Elliot Cohen's *Commentary* magazine.

25. *Judith*, pp. 305-306.

26. Ibid., p. 311. One possible approach to the story was suggested by Meyer Schapiro in an August 7, 1974, letter to Wald: "I couldn't help thinking of Max Eastman when I read the story (he spoke at the Hippodrome meeting) but also of his son Daniel, who was a member of the Trotsky party in 1937. F. [Farrell] later regretted his own attacks on Eastman and the story is perhaps a kind of restitution, in which the Trotskyist son becomes a Stalinist." Tom Carroll does resemble Eastman in his physical appearance, although other aspects of his character and life are quite different.

Chapter 4: The Line of Blood

1. Hook, *John Dewey*, p. 375. The speech was given at the Mecca Temple and is quoted in Farrell's essay, "John Dewey in Mexico."

2. These charges are summarized from Novack's introduction to *The Case of Leon Trotsky*, p. vii.

3. Diary, February 7, 1937.

4. "Comrades: Nu-Style," *Socialist Call* (October 10, 1936), 5.

5. "I Support Thomas," *Socialist Call* (October 24, 1936), 12.

6. JTF to Elizabeth, October 21, 1936. The letter also mentions that Farrell has been "warned" against coming out for Trotsky.

7. "The Nation and Trotsky," *New Masses*, 21 (November 16, 1936), 11-12.

8. These are the conclusions of Warren's *Liberals and Communism*, which my own research tends to confirm.

9. *Southern Review*, 3 (Autumn 1937), 406.

10. "Migratory Intellectuals," *New Masses,* 21 (December 16, 1936), 27-29.
11. Among other things, the meeting voted not to include the names of Cannon and Shachtman on the letterhead of the Committee, in order to prevent the Stalinists from using the fact as ammunition. See diary, November 13, 1936.
12. McCarthy, *On the Contrary,* 95.
13. Diary, November 18, 1936.
14. Morrow to Wald, May 29, 1974.
15. Novack to Wald, July 8, 1974.
16. As reported in a letter of August 9, 1974 to Wald, Harold and Viola Isaacs were quite active on the Committee, writing press releases and doing miscellaneous chores. Isaacs considered his work for the Committee to be his major activity during his association with the Trotskyist movement. In a letter to Wald of August 19, 1974, Suzanne La Follette states that her association with the Committee was strictly limited to collaboration in the establishment of the Commission of Inquiry and publication of its findings.
17. Adamic, *My America,* pp. 72-89; Halper, *Good-bye, Union Square,* pp. 141-143.
18. Both quotations are from Adamic, *My America,* p. 85.
19. Deutscher, *The Prophet Outcast,* p. 357.
20. Undated diary entry for early February, 1937.
21. JTF to Norman Thomas, January 31, 1937.
22. *Socialist Call* (January 2, 1937), 10.
23. *Socialist Call* (February 13, 1937), 4; *New Republic,* 140 (February 24, 1937), 75.
24. Correspondence between Dewey and Farrell in the Farrell Collection shows that Dewey had some hesitancy about undertaking the responsibility at first.
25. Novack, *The Case of Leon Trotsky,* p. viii.
26. The full membership of the Preliminary Commission consisted of John Dewey, Otto Rühle (a noted German Socialist), Stolberg, La Follette, Carleton Beals (an authority on Latin America), Alfred Rosmer, Wendelin Thomas (who had been a leader of the Wilhelmshaven Sailors Revolt in 1918), Edward A. Ross (Professor of Sociology at the University of Wisconsin), John Chamberlain, and Carlo Tresca. The first five comprised the special Subcommission. John Finerty, famed for his defense work in the Tom Mooney and Sacco-Vanzetti cases, was the Commission's legal counsel, and Albert Goldman was Trotsky's attorney. Sister committees existed in France, England, and Czechoslovakia.
27. Diary, February 7, 1937.
28. Diary, February 9, 1937. Also see JTF to Wald, January 21, 1974, and JTF to Lundberg, December 27, 1937.

29. *New Masses,* 22 (February 16, 1937), 1.
30. Diary, February 21, 1937.
31. Diary, March 3, 1937. That evening Farrell attended a meeting of the Trotsky Defense Committee at which Dewey was present. He recorded that also present was "the Trotskyist dissenter [B. J.] Field who, as expected, dissented."
32. *New Masses,* 22 (March 2, 1937), 9.
33. Diary, March 18, 1937.
34. Diary, March 22, 1937.
35. Mrs. Abel had worked as an assistant to James Cannon.
36. Diary, March 23, 1937.
37. Diary, March 28, 1937. Also see JTF to Wald, January 21, 1974.
38. Diary, March 30, 1937. Farrell also noted that James Rorty stated that "they [the Trotskyists] used the same methods here as in the dissolution of the Non-Partisan Labor Defense." Farrell remarked that during the debate over Hays, "George [Novack] got evangelical. He's a combination of intelligence, adoration for Trotsky, respect for big names."
39. JTF to Wald, January 21, 1974. Farrell recollected that on the trip to Mexico, during a stop-off in St. Louis, Stolberg wanted Farrell to agree to let him send his vote back to Rorty, along with Suzanne La Follette's and his own, to take over the Committee and oust or put into a place of no influence the Trotskyist party members. Farrell refused. Suzanne La Follette's recollection, however, is that no competition or friction existed between Farrell and Stolberg. La Follette to Wald, August 19, 1974.
40. "Dewey in Mexico," in Hook, *John Dewey,* pp. 351-377; and "A Memoir of Trotsky," *University of Kansas City Review,* 23 (Summer 1957), 293-298.
41. JTF to Marshall, April 16, 1937.
42. "A Memoir of Trotsky," *University of Kansas City Review,* 23 (Summer 1957), 296.
43. *New Masses,* 23 (April 20, 1937), 28. A week later the attack continued with "Inside the Trotsky Trial," *New Masses,* 23 (April 27, 1937), 6-12. On May 18, the *New Masses* carried a report that Waldo Frank had proposed a new investigating commission, but that during a meeting at the Mecca Temple, Stolberg had told him bluntly that he could forget about the idea. See *New Masses,* 23 (May 18, 1937), 10-11.
44. JTF to Patchen, May 10, 1937. The letter also contained the following: "It gets more and more impossible for them [the Stalinists] to conduct any polemics or disagreements on a decent plane. Only recently I received a clipping from the *New York Times,* a dispatch under a Moscow date line of April 26. The last paragraph referred to an article written in a Russian periodical by one Sidney Blumfield— the name is unknown to me. It dealt with a notorious gang of

American writers, and this band was described as a band of 'Trotskyist Robbers of the Pen.' It listed myself with Max Eastman, Calverton, Sidney Hook, etc., including Isaac Don Levine, a Hearst writer, with whom I have nothing in common. This is symptomatic and indicative of where one ends when one gets entangled in that system."

45. *Saturday Review of Literature,* 16 (June 5, 1937), 10, 14.
46. *Southern Review,* 3 (Summer 1937), 207-208. Schuman answered Farrell and Farrell rebutted in *Southern Review,* 3 (Autumn 1937), 406-416. The same section on "Correspondence" contains an exchange between Sidney Hook and Carleton Beals on Beals' walkout and denunciation of the hearings. Dewey and other members of the Commission felt that Beals had intentionally asked provocative questions and then quit the hearings, as a response to direct or indirect pressure from the Stalinists. See "Confidential Report, Mexico, April 15, 1937," in possession of George Novack.
47. See the following issues of the *Socialist Call:* July 10, 1937, 5; July 17, 1937, 4; July 24, 1937, 5; July 31, 1937, 5; August 7, 1937, 5; August 14, 1937, 5; August 21, 1937, 5; August 28, 1937, 5; September 4, 1937, 5; September 11, 1937, 5.
48. Diary, May 31, 1937. (However, in an August 13, 1974 letter to Wald, Clark states that she doesn't recall this meeting.) A number of these same individuals also had ties with the Trotsky Defense Committee. For example, on June 4, 1937, Farrell recorded a June 3rd meeting at which Solow and Rorty were present (along with the Trotskyists Novack and Isaacs). At that gathering the Committee decided to accept Harper's terms for publication of the record of the Commission's proceedings, although Farrell noted that, in general, there seemed to be a lull in the Committee's activities.
49. Hart, *Writers in a Changing World,* p. 28. In an undated June entry in his Diary, Farrell also mentions that the Trotskyist and poet Sherry Mangan attended the Congress—although there is no record of what Mangan said or did, if anything.
50. Diary, June, day not given, 1937.
51. JTF to Wald, January 24, 1974.
52. Diary, July 29, 1937. On August 8, Farrell recorded having sent a letter to Albert Glotzer, a Trotskyist leader in Chicago, regarding a matter of internal party discipline.
53. Diary, August 23, 1937.
54. See diary, December 31, 1936. On January 6, 1937, Farrell noted that Phillips was still hesitating over the break with the Stalinists, and that he and Rahv continued to find arguments to the effect that the Trotskyists were incorrect and ineffective. On January 22, 1937, Farrell noted that Phillips and Rahv had "backed out" of the meeting with Norman Thomas. Differences with them over political

and literary tactics seem to have persisted throughout the spring and fall. In an undated entry for June or early July 1937, Farrell noted that Rahv and Phillips decided against printing Max Eastman in the new magazine for "strategical" reasons. In a November 30, 1937 entry, Farrell records his objection to a decision made by *Partisan Review* not to publish an article by Andre Gide because it was "too political."

55. Novack to Wald, June 24, 1974.
56. Interview with William Phillips, November, 1973.
57. *Socialist Call* (September 18, 1937), 5. A year later Farrell also defended *Partisan Review* against criticism from Malcolm Cowley. See *New Republic*, 147 (November 30, 1938), 103-104.
58. *Saturday Review of Literature*, 17 (December 25, 1937), 19.
59. *New Masses*, 23 (May 11, 1937), 22 (see poem about Suzanne La Follette). See also *New Masses*, 27 (April 12, 1938), 84-86, for a poem by Granville Hicks called "Revolution in Bohemia." This tells how a radical intellectual gets into the clutches of Calverton, Eastman, Eugene Lyons and Trotsky, and ends up supporting the bourgeoisie.
60. *New Masses*, 26 (December 28, 1937), 9.
61. *New Masses*, 26 (January 4, 1938), 16.
62. *New Masses*, 26 (January 18, 1938), 11.
63. *New Masses*, 26 (February 1, 1938), 12.
64. Ibid., 14.
65. *New Masses*, 26 (February 15, 1938), 3.
66. Interview with Farrell, November 1973.
67. Diary, January 15, 1939. On January 16 Farrell recorded that he had a conversation with Novack, who completely defended the Shachtman-Burnham article. Another conflict with Novack was recorded a few months later on May 4, 1939. Farrell noted that he had been questioning Novack about Trotskyist policy toward the American Labor party and *New Leader*. He felt that the answers were not satisfactory and commented that "George is dogmatic."
68. Farrell records his participation in his diary entries of January 15, March 18 (where twenty-eight people were present), and October 27, 1939. On November 2 Farrell noted that Dwight Macdonald, Secretary of the League, had sent a letter to Sidney Hook's more recently formed competitor organization, the League for Cultural Freedom, asking for cooperation between the two groups in defense of the French conservative novelist John Giono. Farrell was also disturbed about the fact that the Trotskyist newspaper *Socialist Appeal* was excluded from the Reporters' Table at a recent conference of Hook's group.
69. See the articles in *Socialist Appeal* (February 24, 1939), 1, including Felix Morrow's "All Races, Creeds Join Picket Line."

70. *Socialist Appeal* (February 20, 1939), 3. See also JTF to Thomas, February 26, 1939.
71. In Farrell's diary, on June 11, he describes a baseball game between his Studs Lonigan A.C. and the Marxist Maulers (probably members of the Socialist Workers party). Farrell recorded that the game ended in a nine to nine tie, and that at one point the game was almost ruined because Felix Morrow lost his temper. However, in a letter to Wald on January 21, 1974, Farrell corrected what was an apparent error: "The game did not end in a tie. I hit a ball into the gallery that drove in the winning run."
72. Diary, October 9, 1939.
73. Diary, October 30, 1939. In the same entry, Farrell also noted that Max Nomad had recently said that Trotsky was "the greatest man alive."
74. Diary, November 5, November 12, 1939. Farrell does not elaborate his comments on Goldman. However, in the major document of the Shachtman-Burnham faction it is mentioned that Goldman had supported them on previous occasions, and then had suddenly switched sides. See Cannon, *The Struggle for a Proletarian Party*, p. 276.
75. Diary, December 1, 1939, and December 10, 1939. The December 9, 1939 entry also discusses aspects of the dispute. The two articles by Trotsky have been reprinted in *In Defense of Marxism*.
76. Interview with Farrell, November 1973.
77. Farrell, *An Omnibus of Short Stories*, p. 195.
78. In Farrell's diary entry for August 11, 1939, he noted that both Phillips and Rahv liked the book; and on October 8 he received a note from Thomas Mann praising it. However, Babbette Deutsch's review in *Partisan Review*, 7 (Winter 1940), 72-73, was mixed. She concluded that in spite of its "verisimilitude," the book "wants cogency." In an unpublished manuscript in the Farrell Collection, Farrell notes that John Dewey considered the short novel "a classic."
79. Farrell noted that Wright's use of accident and coincidence presented a "sense of racial effects of the patterns of lynch law." *Partisan Review*,4 (May 1938), 57-58.
80. *Saturday Review of Literature*, 18 (August 13, 1938), 12. It should be noted that the argument of this review is strikingly less partisan than other writings of Farrell on the trials.
81. *Southern Review*, 4 (Spring 1939), 771-783.
82. *Partisan Review*, 6 (Summer 1939), 607-610.
83. Broun called Farrell reactionary in the *New Republic*, 149 (June 28, 1939), 213; Farrell repeated his criticisms of the Second American Writers' Congress, charging Stalinist domination, lack of democracy, an acquiescence to the coming war, and a refusal to distinguish

between serious and commercial writing. The full text of Farrell's answer is in *Socialist Appeal* (July 28, 1939), 3.

84. *American Mercury,* 97 (August 1939), 489-94. The correspondence between Dos Passos and Farrell in the Farrell Collection shows that Dos Passos was appreciative of Farrell's support, and also that Dos Passos especially liked Farrell's novels *Gas-House McGinty, Ellen Rogers,* and *Father and Son.*

85. *Nation,* 149 (September 30, 1939), 359. The editors replied that it was the Stalinists who had to explain their positions and not the *Nation;* and that the *Nation* had, in fact, "strongly and clearly attacked the Soviet Trials."

86. *American Mercury,* 48 (November 1939), 381-382.

87. Farrell was writing here with characteristic objectivity, for Roth, Algren and Dahlberg were all writers who had been, in varying degrees, pro-Stalinist and in conflict with Farrell.

88. *American Mercury,* 48 (December 1939), 408-414.

Chapter 5: Standing Fast

1. Schapiro to JTF, August 25, 1940.

2. Farrell reviewed Levine's book on the Trotsky assassination many years later. See *Saturday Review of Literature* 43 (January 23, 1960), 32-33.

3. Paul Jacobs' Trotskyist memoir, *Is Curley Jewish?,* gives a feeling for the impact of the murder on those close to the movement. See pp. 108-109.

4. The demoralizing effects of the faction fight for some Trotskyists were indicated in a letter from Harold Isaacs to Wald, August 9, 1974. Isaacs reported that although he and his wife supported the Cannon faction "passively," they no longer felt the movement viable.

5. *Partisan Review,* 7 (March-April 1940), pp. 139-42. Farrell's second installment of "The Cultural Front" was a satire on liberals like Lewis Mumford and Archibald MacLeish. See *Partisan Review,* 7 (July-August 1940), 311-313.

6. JTF to Mary Farrell, August 26, 1940. A letter to Farrell from William Phillips around the same time expresses very similar emotions and calls for an "intellectual pogrom" against Stalinism.

7. *Labor Action* (September 2, 1940), 2; *Socialist Appeal* (September 7, 1940), 3; *Partisan Review,* 7 (September-October 1940), 388-390.

8. *New Republic,* 103 (October 28, 1940), 595-596. A similar kind of review is Granville Hicks' "The Longevity of Integrity," in *Saturday Review of Literature,* 47 (June 20, 1964), 31-32. Hicks was reviewing

What Time Collects, admitting that he had not bothered to read its predecessor in the new series by Farrell, *The Silence of History.* After Farrell became "typed" as a certain kind of writer, he often received somewhat shabby treatment from critics who should have known better.

9. Newton Berry, "A Preface to the Death Fantasy Sequence of Judgment Day," *Triquarterly,* I (Winter 1965), 124. What remained after the fire was published in ibid., 127-138.

10. *Partisan Review,* 7 (November-December 1940), 435-455.

11. *Partisan Review,* 8 (January-February 1941), 78-79.

12. Interview with Farrell, November 1973. Farrell said that he did not know exactly all the reasons behind these incidents, but tended to associate petty things with the way the editors worked.

13. Rahv to JTF, March 18, 1941.

14. Interview with William Phillips, November 1973.

15. Interview with Dwight Macdonald, November 1973.

16. *Partisan Review,* 8 (July-August 1941), 349.

17. George Novack's "Introduction" to *Socialism on Trial,* pp. 10-11.

18. According to Felix Morrow, the courtroom strategy was entirely worked out by the Trotskyist attorney Albert Goldman, who was also one of the eighteen convicted. (Morrow to Wald, August 12, 1974.) However, this recollection was disputed in a May 1976 interview with George Breitman. Breitman recalls that the strategy was hashed out in the Political Committee of the Socialist Workers party, of which he was a member.

19. This press statement appeared in the *Militant* (September 20, 1941), 1. Two other documents in Farrell's possession gave further information on preparatory stages: an August 20, 1941 ACLU "Protest to Attorney-General Biddle on the Minnesota Indictments," and an elaborate September 12 statement on structural proposals for the CRDC signed by Novack. A personal letter from Novack to Farrell, sent in early September, indicated that there had been a hope of obtaining John Dewey for honorary chairman: "Dewey will join the Committee, but he didn't want to be one of the initiators on the grounds that the leading figures should be different from those in the Trotsky defense. From the 200 or more liberal and labor leaders that we asked to join, maybe we will get another, and perhaps even better, Honorary Chairman."

20. CRDC Statement of Income, July 24 to October 3, 1941.

21. JTF to Matt and Helen, October 29, 1941.

22. An introduction for Novack's pamphlet *Witch Hunt in Minnesota,* had been requested of Dos Passos, but Farrell ended up writing it. The pamphlet was published by the Civil Rights Defense Committee in 1941, and Farrell's introduction appears on pp. 3 and 4.

23. Novack, *Defense Policies and Principles of the Socialist Workers Party*, p. 9. See also a memo of April 29 (the year is not indicated, but it was probably 1942) from Evelyn Reed to JTF, explaining that, on the one hand, Dos Passos had never come up with an article he promised to write; but, on the other hand, he had promptly responded to a request for autographed books for CRDC fundraising. The selection of Dos Passos's letters in *The Fourteenth Chronicle* contains no references to the Minneapolis Case.

24. JTF to Helen, November 13, 1941.

25. Novack to JTF, September 15, 1941. In late 1937 Leon Trotsky had addressed a letter to James Cannon, Max Shachtman and George Novack, expressing his concern that the Trotsky Defense Committee, composed mainly of intellectuals, be augmented by "delegates of workers groups. . . ." Trotsky later expressed dismay that this wasn't done. See Trotsky, *In Defense of Marxism*, p. 10.

26. Novack to JTF, September 25, 1941.

27. Novack to JTF, October 7, 1941. Grant Dunne was one of the Minneapolis Dunne brothers, noted for their militancy. Three of the brothers became Trotskyist union leaders, and a fourth, Bill Dunne, was for many years a Communist party official. Grant Dunne had attempted suicide previously, but the successful attempt may have been linked to despondency about possible confinement.

28. Novack to JTF, October 18, 1941. A letter from Reed to Hortense Farrell dated October 17, 1941, discusses other recent news articles on the case.

29. Reprinted in the *Militant* (December 27, 1941), 2.

30. See letters from Reed to JTF on June 9, 1942, and from Jules Geller to JTF on August 31, 1942. Both request that Farrell write replies for financial contributions to the CRDC. Farrell himself was a regular donor. See the November 14, 1942 letter from Reed to JTF concerning money raised by Farrell's autographed books, and also a December 28, 1942 letter from Geller to Farrell requesting more autographed books.

31. See July 18, 1942 letter from Reed to Hortense and JTF. Although Novack served the Socialist Workers party primarily through his writing and work on defense committees, this phase of industrial work was probably inspired by the proletarianization policy of the 1940 Political Resolution (at the convention where the split between Cannon and Shachtman occurred): "The entire party membership must be directed toward rooting itself in the factories, mills, etc., and towards integrating itself into the unions and workers' mass organizations." Reprinted in Cannon, *The Struggle for a Proletarian Party*, p. 236. Also, men Novack's age were not being drafted if they were employed in industries deemed necessary to national defense.

32. That same summer, Meyer Schapiro wrote JTF criticizing Novack's orthodox Marxist critique of Sidney Hook. ("The Degradation of Sidney Hook," *Fourth International*, 3 [June 1942], 174-177, under the pseudonym of William F. Warde.)

33. *Militant* (January 16, 1943), 1. See also Novack's article on Tresca in the *Militant* (January 23, 1943), 3, and Farrell's "In Remembrance of Carlo Tresca," *Militant* (May 1, 1943), 4. *An American Dream Girl* (1950) is dedicated by Farrell "To Margaret De Silver and to the Memory of Carlo Tresca."

34. See December 28, 1942 letter from Attorney-General Biddle to Post-Master General; also, January 23, 1943 protest of Morris Milgram from the Workers Defense League. Copies in Farrell Collection.

35. February 2, 1943 letter from Novack to JTF to all CRDC National Committee members.

36. *Militant* (February 20, 1943), 1.

37. *Nation*, 157 (September 11, 1943), 307.

38. Farrell's involvement is indicated in the following: "The Story Behind Kelly Postal's Conviction," *Shall Kelly Postal Go to Prison for His Loyalty to Trade Union Democracy?*, by Farrell and Novack (New York: Civil Rights Defense Committee, 1943); "Kelly Postal's Conviction," by Farrell, *Militant* (March 3, 1943), 3; "The Story Behind Kelly Postal's Frame-Up," by Farrell (a Civil Rights Defense Committee leaflet, 1943). Also see the following letters: JTF to Dorothy Schultz of the Workers Defense League, February 2, 1943; Reed to JTF, February 5, 1943; Novack to JTF, March 1, 1943; Reed to JTF, March 11, 1943; Reed to JTF, March 15, 1943; Reed to JTF, July 28, 1943; Reed to JTF, October 28, 1943; Reed to JTF, November 8, 1943; Reed to JTF, November 16, 1943; Reed to JTF, November 17, 1943.

39. Reed to JTF, June 21, 1943.

40. Reed to JTF, July 26, 1943.

41. Reed to JTF, December 7, 1943; *Militant* (September 25, 1943), 1; *Labor Action* (October 4, 1943), 2; *Militant* (December 4, 1943), 1-2;) *Militant* (December 25, 1943), 3.

42. *Militant* (January 1, 1944), 3.

43. Reed to JTF, January 2, 1944.

44. *Socialist Call* (January 7, 1944), 1; Radio speech on WEVD, New York City, April 15, 1944; *New Republic*, 110 (May 29, 1944), 740; *Militant* (June 17, 1944); *Militant* (September 9, 1944), 1; Speech at Manhattan Center, October 27, 1944.

45. See the following letters from Reed to JTF: January 3, 1944; February 1, 1944; February 8, 1944; May 19, 1944; June 1, 1944; June 27, 1944; July 5, 1944; August 7, 1944; August 22, 1944; August 29, 1944; September 14, 1944; September 21, 1944; October 25,

1944; December 22, 1944; December 27, 1944. See also Novack to JTF, May 1, 1944.

46. "News from the Prisoners in the Minneapolis Labor Case," Press Release, February 15, 1944.

47. Cannon, *Letters from Prison*, p. 52. On July 10, 1944, Cannon also wrote: "I read [James T.] Farrell's piece on Ring Lardner. He is a good critic as well as creator, a combination not seen too often. I wonder if Jim [Farrell] doesn't read more consciousness and design into Lardner than Lardner knew about. I recall the baseball stories as rich humor," ibid., p. 114

48. "News from the Prisoners in the Minneapolis Labor Case," Press Release, February 15, 1944.

49. *Who Are the 18 Prisoners in the Minneapolis Labor Case*, Civil Rights Defense Committee pamphlet, 1944.

Chapter 6: The Lonely Decade

1. *The Silence of History*, p. 159.

2. The scope of this study does not permit a discussion of other concerns, such as Farrell's friendship with H. L. Mencken. In an April 23, 1942 letter to Mencken, Farrell discussed plans for a political novel based on the life of Al Smith.

3. JTF to Henle, January 30, 1942.

4. JTF to Schapiro, July 31, 1942.

5. Schapiro to JTF, July 10, 1942.

6. JTF to Schapiro, July 14, 1942.

7. Schapiro to Wald, February 18, 1974.

8. Schapiro to JTF, July 31, 1942.

9. Schapiro to JTF, July 25, 1942.

10. JTF to Schapiro, August 3, 1942.

11. JTF to Dunne, November 1, 1942.

12. JTF to Switalski, April 5, 1943. Switalski was a friend of Farrell's from the Chicago days.

13. The letter to Goldman was printed in Trotsky's *In Defense of Marxism*, p. 184.

14. JTF to Switalski, April 20, 1943. Farrell believed that Hook's *Partisan Review* reference to "irresponsible half-drunk cocktail blusterers who take no responsibility in it" was an attack on himself, according to a letter to Switalski, April 5, 1943. The quotation cited from Farrell about Hook is only one representative of a large quantity of anti-Hook comments contained in Farrell's correspondence of this period.

15. *Partisan Review*, 10 (January-February 1943), 2-23.

16. JTF to Switalski, June 24, 1943. In an earlier unsent letter to Hook,

Farrell declared Dewey to be simply "not radical." JTF to Hook, October 28, 1939.
17. JTF to Schapiro, June 24, 1943.
18. JTF to Schapiro, June 27, 1943.
19. JTF to Switalski, July 28, 1943.
20. JTF to Wald, February 5, 1974. See also the following letters: JTF to Rosmer, May 27, 1944; Natalia Trotsky to JTF, May 10, 1944. (In her letters Natalia Trotsky laments that she does not know English sufficiently to read Farrell's books.) Also see the untitled and undated manuscript by Farrell on great women in the Farrell Collection.
21. *Southern Review*, 6 (Winter 1941), 417-438; *Partisan Review*, 9 (January-February 1942), 38-47; *College English*, 3 (April 1942), 611-623; *New Republic*, 111 (December 4, 1944), 764, 766-769. (All of the above except the *Partisan Review* piece are reprinted in *The League of Frightened Philistines*.)
22. Farrell, "Literature and Ideology," *The League of Frightened Philistines*, p. 19; *Leon Trotsky on Literature and Art*, p. 106.
23. *Partisan Review*, 9 (May-June 1942), 203-212. See also the correction in *Partisan Review*, 9 (July-August 1942), 353, and Farrell's apology to Max Eastman in *Partisan Review*, 17 (July-August 1950), 630. Farrell had also engaged in a previous argument with Eastman, reflected in a private letter from JTF to Eastman dated October 11, 1939. Nevertheless, despite the battles, correspondence between Eastman and Farrell indicates that they remained friends, and Eliena Eastman wrote to Hortense Farrell as well. In an unpublished manuscript, Farrell recalls first seeing Eastman at a party in Eastman's honor in 1933. Farrell holds the opinion that the second volume of Eastman's autobiography, *Love and Revolution*, was treated unfairly by some reviewers.
24. Farrell, *The League of Frightened Philistines*, xi; *Leon Trotsky on Literature and Art*, p. 111.
25. Farrell, *The League of Frightened Philistines*, p. xii.
26. *New International*, 13 (April 1947), 111-114. Farrell argued that the book expressed a tendency to show the hero not as an actor but as an observer with penetrating powers, and he suggested it was symptomatic of the coming of a "New Gentility" in fiction.
27. In *Triquarterly*,1 (Winter 1965), 139, Farrell listed a number of critics whom he believed had warred against his works, including Irving Howe. Howe answered that all he had ever done was write "a brief, though admittedly severe note on Farrell's criticism." See *Triquarterly*, No. 4 (1965), 198-199. At least one critic who, in opposition to Howe, lauded Farrell for maintaining critical sanity in the 1940s, was Harry Levin. See "Tell It Not in Gath," *New Republic*, 113 (July 23, 1945), 105-106. Another who took a different view from Howe of the same

critical works was Harry Sylvester in "Righteous Anger," *New Republic*, 117 (October 26, 1947), 26-27.

28. *Partisan Review*, 14 (September-October 1947), 545-546, 548, 550, 552. The correspondence between Howe and Farrell shows that earlier in the 1940s Howe had been a great admirer of Farrell, and that Farrell had helped Howe obtain publications outside of the Workers party press. In one letter, Howe even praised Farrell's critique of Trilling's "The Other Margaret."

29. "A Comment on Literature and Morality," *New International*, 12 (May 1946), 141-145; reprinted in *Literature and Morality*. Also see the interesting debate between Farrell and Howard Mumford Jones in the following articles: Jones, "A Code for Art," *Saturday Review of Literature*, 30 (September 6, 1947), 18-19; Farrell, "The Sovereign Pen," *Saturday Review of Literature*, 30 (December 20, 1947), 21-22. Another critic who interpreted Farrell's views on morality incorrectly was Charles Glicksberg in *Southern Review*, 11 (Summer 1950), 189-196.

30. Kempton, *Part of Our Time*, pp. 128-129. It's worth noting that some left-wing critics have come up with some rather dubious theories to explain their dislike of or disagreement with Farrell's fiction, although Kempton is not in this group. Irving Howe (writing under the pseudonym R. Fangston in *New International*, 8 [July 1942], 182-184) speculated that Farrell's art was declining due to a lack of financial security in the 1940s, while Peter Clecak (at one time associated with *Monthly Review*) wrote in the *Nation*, 182 (June 3, 1968), 733-734, that Farrell's alleged decline was because his personal success had cancelled out the need for his socialist politics.

31. Farrell was continually educating himself; for example, in 1941 he took a course in mathematical logic and received an "A." This was mentioned in the *New York Times* (December 3, 1967), 138.

32. "James T. Farrell: Beyond the Provinces of Art," *New World Writing*, 5 (April 1954), 60.

33. Reprinted in *Literature and Morality* with related essays on Tolstoy.

34. In an interview in *Bookweek*, October 25, 1964, pp. 6 and 23, Farrell stated the following of *Invisible Swords:* "It's the most powerful book I've ever written." Among many indications of the importance to Farrell of the fears he indicated in "The Fate of Writing in America" was the debate he had with James M. Cain, recorded in the article "Do Writers Need an AAA?", *Saturday Review of Literature*, 29 (November 16, 1946), 9, 10, 44, 45, 47. Farrell's ongoing battle against censorship is evidenced in articles such as "On Zola and Mr. McCann," *New Leader*, 33 (May 13, 1950), 21-22.

35. *New International*, 12 (April 1946), 112-115; *New Republic*, 114 (April 29, 1946), 616, 618; *New Republic*, 114 (May 13, 1946), 702, 704-705.

The latter two are reprinted in *Literature and Morality*, pp. 168-176.

36. *English Journal*, 35 (June 1936), 309-315; *Literature and Morality*, pp. 15-25.
37. *New International*, 12 (September 1946), 218-223; *New International*, 12 (October 1946), 243-247.
38. *New International*, 13 (January 1947), 20-27.
39. *New International*, 13 (March 1947), 86-89.
40. *New International*, 13 (December 1947), 278-279; *New International*, 14 (January 1948), 21-24; *New International*, 14 (February 1948), 40-41; *New International*, 14 (March 1948), 78-80; *New International*, 14 (April 1948), 120-123.
41. *Humanist*, 7 (Autumn 1947), 57-63; *Humanist*, 7 (Winter 1947), 114-118.
42. Novack to Wald, April 29, 1973.
43. Interview with Novack, November, 1973.
44. The political dispute is one of the central themes of the letters collected in Cannon's *Letters from Prison*. Also, see volumes 7 and 8 of the Socialist Workers party's *Internal Bulletin*—especially volume 8, no. 7, containing charges and answers about the Goldman-Morrow group's involvement with the Workers party. Participants in the dispute are often referred to by the following pseudonyms: Morrow (Cassidy), Goldman (Morrison), Cannon (Martin), Farrell (O'Neal), Novack (Warde).
45. See the following: "How the Trotskyists Went to Jail," *Fourth International*, 5 (February 1944), 43; "A Defamer of Marxism," *Fourth International*, 5 (May 1944), 149; "The Only Moral People," *Politics*, 1 (May 1944); "James T. Farrell and the S.W.P.," *Politics*, 1 (December 1944), 351-352.
46. *Politics*, 2 (July 1945).
47. *New International*, 11 (August 1945), 144-148.
48. JTF to Novack, October 12, 1945.
49. JTF to Novack, July 1 and July 7, 1945.
50. JTF to Novack, February 24, 1946.
51. Farrell had heard that although Natalia Trotsky had requested the Socialist Workers party to undertake this kind of project, they had refused—even though the Trotskyists in England were undertaking it.
52. March 8 and March 10, 1947. The first appears to be a preliminary draft. Farrell argues that: (1) The Socialist Workers party had suddenly changed its view of anti-Stalinist "informers," having previously denounced Ruth Fischer and now taking advantage of some of Louis Budenz's revelations; (2) Farrell believed that he was abused whenever he disagreed with the Socialist Workers party, but courted when his name was needed.
53. *Politics*, 3 (March 1946), 89-92. The dispute is continued with Nicola

Chiarmonte in *Politics,* 3 (May 1946), 168-170. For Lionel Abel's description of a verbal sally between Farrell and Chiarmonte, see *Commentary,* 56 (July 1973), 26.

54. *Labor Action* (May 17, 1948), 3.
55. *Socialist Call* (October 29, 1948), 2.
56. *Socialist Call* (September 17, 1948), 2.
57. *Socialist Call* (October 8, 1948), 4. However, a few months later Farrell endorsed the defense case of James Kutcher, a legless veteran of World War II who was fired from his Veterans Administration job because of his Trotskyist views. See *Militant* (April 4, 1949), 4.
58. Delivered at the Grand Ampitheatre of the Sorbonne, April 30, 1949; printed in October 1949, by the Rand School Press, along with the text of an address by Farrell over Voice of America.
59. *New Leader,* 33 (June 24, 1950), 15.
60. Farrell expressed such a view in an undated, untitled manuscript which is in the Farrell Collection.

Chapter 7: The Literary Record

1. *Judith and Other Stories,* p. xi.
2. *Yet Other Waters,* p. 10.
3. *When Boyhood Dreams Come True,* p. 149.
4. Unpublished manuscript, Farrell Collection.
5. This is especially true of "The Martyr."
6. In *American Communism in Crisis,* Starobin writes: "Freeman . . . was editor of the *New Masses* during the Moscow Trials; he made the mistake of allowing his correspondent in the Soviet Union, Joshua Kunitz, leeway to voice doubts about what was happening. A blast from the Comintern attacked Freeman's book [*An American Testament*] as disrespectful to Stalin, among other sins. Freeman was quietly ousted from the Party in 1939." See pp. 253-254.
7. See "The Dialectic," *The Life Adventurous,* pp. 170-182.
8. As Malcolm Cowley noted, many characters in *Yet Other Waters* can be partially identified by use of records from the American Writers' Congresses. See *New Republic,* 127 (December 1, 1952), 17-18.
9. Sanders, *Pattern of Rejection,* p. 266.
10. *Partisan Review,* 7 (September-October 1940), 390.
11. The significance of the character Jim O'Neill was captured in Stephen Vincent Benet's review of *Father and Son* in the *Saturday Review of Literature,* 23 (October 12, 1940), 40.
12. *Childhood Is Not Forever,* pp. 18-54.
13. *Sound of a City,* pp. 27-36.
14. See the following: *Side Street,* pp. 205-212; *Judith and Other Stories,* pp. 131-154; *An American Dream Girl,* pp. 64-72.

15. *An American Dream Girl,* pp. 274-302.
16. *When Boyhood Dreams Come True,* pp. 171-256.
17. See the following: *Sound of a City,* pp. 55-60; *Childhood Is Not Forever,* pp. 194-204; ibid., pp. 77-100, ibid., pp. 1-17; *When Boyhood Dreams Come True,* pp. 134-141.
18. Madden, *Talks With Authors,* p. 94.
19. "How Our Day Began," *The Smith,* 3 (February 15, 1968), 9.

Chapter 8: Conclusion

1. See the following discussions of Harrison's book: Irving Howe, "Beliefs of the Masters," *Decline of the New,* pp. 34-42; George A. Panichas, "The Writer and Society: Some Reflections," *The Politics of Twentieth Century Novelists,* pp. xxxvi-xlv; Philip Rahv, "An Open Secret," *Literature and the Sixth Sense,* pp. 437-445.
2. Alfred Kazin, "The Writer as Political Crazy," *Playboy,* 20 (June 1973), 107-108, 136, 206-209.
3. Of course, many attempts have been made to explain the reasons for this development. Two of the best are the following: David Caute, *The Fellow-Travelers: A Postscript to the Enlightenment,* and George Novack, "Radical Intellectuals in the 1930's," *International Socialist Review,* 29 (March-April 1968), 21-34.
4. Kempton, *Part of Our Time,* p. 128.
5. Schapiro to Wald, August 7, 1974.
6. "An Introduction to Two Novels," *University of Kansas City Review,* 13 (Spring 1947), 218.

Bibliography

The bibliography lists the major books and dissertations consulted, along with those articles not cited in the footnotes.

Adamic, Louis. *My America.* New York: Harper and Brothers, 1938.

Aaron, Daniel. *Writers on the Left.* New York: Avon, 1962.

Beach, Joseph Warren. *American Fiction, 1920-1940.* New York: Macmillan, 1941.

Bell, Daniel. *Marxian Socialism in the U.S.* Princeton: Princeton University Press, 1967.

Bendiner, Robert. *Just Around the Corner.* New York: Harper and Row, 1967.

Branch, Edgar. "American Writer in the Twenties:James T. Farrell and the University of Chicago." *American Book Collector,* 11 (Summer 1961), 25-32.

———. *A Bibliography of James T. Farrell's Writings, 1921-1957.* Philadelphia: University of Pennsylvania Press, 1959.

———. "A Supplement to the Bibliography of James T. Farrell's Writings." *American Book Collector,* 11 (Summer 1961), 42-48.

———. "Bibliography of James T. Farrell: A Supplement." *American Book Collector,* 12 (May 1967), 9-19.

172

———. "Bibliography of James T. Farrell: January, 1967 - August, 1970." *American Book Collector,* 12 (March-April 1971), 13-18.

———. *James T. Farrell.* New York: Twayne Publishers, 1971.

———. "The 1930s in James T. Farrell's Fiction." *American Book Collector,* 21 (March-April 1971), 9-12.

Burnett, James Thomas. "American Trotskyism and the Russian Question." Diss. U. C. Berkeley, 1969.

Buhle, Paul M. "Louis C. Fraina, 1892-1953." Master's Thesis, University of Connecticut, 1968.

Cannon, James P. *The First Ten Years of American Communism.* New York: Lyle Stuart, 1962.

———. *The History of American Trotskyism.* New York: Pioneer, 1944.

———. *Letters from Prison.* New York: Merit, 1968.

———. *Notebook of an Agitator.* New York: Pioneer, 1958.

———. *Socialism on Trial.* New York: Merit, 1969.

———. *The Socialist Workers Party in World War II.* New York: Pathfinder, 1975.

———. *The Struggle for a Proletarian Party.* New York: Pioneer, 1943.

———. *The Struggle for Socialism in the "American Century."* New York: Pathfinder, 1977.

Caute, David. *The Fellow-Travellers.* New York: Macmillan, 1973.

Civil Rights Defense Committee. *Who Are the 18 Prisoners in the Minneapolis Case?* New York: Civil Rights Defense Committee, 1944.

Clecak, Peter. "Marxism and American Literary Criticism." Diss. Stanford University, 1964.

Conroy, Jack. *The Disinherited.* New York: Hill and Wang, 1963.

———, and Johnson, Curt, eds. *Writers in Revolt: The Anvil Anthology.* New York: Lawrence Hill and Company, 1973.

Cowley, Malcolm. *Exile's Return.* New York: Viking, 1966.

———. *Think Back on Us: The Literary Record.* Carbondale: Southern Illinois University Press, 1972.

———. *Think Back on Us: The Social Record.* Carbondale: Southern Illinois University Press, 1972.

Crossman, Richard, ed. *The God That Failed.* New York: Bantam, 1965.

Curley, Thomas F. "Catholic Novels and American Culture." *Commentary*, 37 (July 1963), 34-42.

Dahlberg, Edward. *The Confessions of Edward Dahlberg*. New York: George Braziller, 1971.

Deutscher, Isaac. *The Prophet Outcast*. New York: Vintage, 1963.

Diggins, John P. *Up From Communism*, New York: Harper and Row, 1975.

Dos Passos, John. *Adventures of a Young Man*. New York: Harcourt, Brace and Company, 1938.

———. *The Fourteenth Chronicle*. Boston: Gambit Incorporated, 1973.

———. *The Theme Is Freedom*. New York: Dodd, Mead and Company, 1956.

Draper, Theodore. *American Communism and Soviet Russia*. New York: Viking, 1960.

———. *The Roots of American Communism*. New York: Viking, 1957.

Dyer, Henry H. "James T. Farrell's Studs Lonigan and Danny O'Neill Novels." Diss. University of Pennsylvania, 1965.

Eastman, Max. *Love and Revolution*. New York: Random House, 1965.

Eisinger, Chester E. *Fiction of the Forties*. Chicago: University of Chicago Press, 1963.

Fabre, Michel. "Jack Conroy as Editor." *New Letters*, 39 (December 1972), 115-137.

Farrell, James T. *An American Dream Girl*. New York: Vanguard, 1950.

———. *A Brand New Life*. New York: Manor Books, 1973.

———. *Bernard Clare*. New York: Vanguard, 1946.

———. *Boarding House Blues*. New York: Paperback Library, 1961.

———. *Childhood Is Not Forever*. New York: Doubleday and Company, 1969.

———. *The Collected Poems of James T. Farrell*. New York: Fleet Publishing Corporation, 1965.

———. *A Dangerous Woman and Other Stories*. New York: Signet, 1957.

———. *Ellen Rogers*. New York: Sun Dial Press, 1942.

———. *The Face of Time*. New York: Popular Library, 1962.

———. *French Girls Are Vicious*. New York: Vanguard, 1955.

———. *Gas-House McGinty*. Cleveland: World Publishing Company, 1943.

———. *Invisible Swords*. New York: Doubleday, 1971.

———. *Judith and Other Stories.* New York: Doubleday, 1973.

———. *The League of Frightened Philistines.* New York: Vanguard, 1945.

———. *Literature and Morality.* New York: Vanguard, 1947.

———. *Lonely for the Future.* New York: Dell, 1967.

———. *My Days of Anger.* New York: Popular Library, 1961.

———. *New Year's Eve/1929.* New York: The Smith, 1967.

———. *No Star Is Lost.* New York: Popular Library, 1944.

———. *A Note on Literary Criticism.* New York: Vanguard, 1936.

———. *An Omnibus of Short Stories.* New York: Vanguard, 1956.

———. *Reflections at Fifty.* New York: Vanguard, 1954.

———. *The Road Between.* New York: Vanguard, 1949.

———. *The Short Stories of James T. Farrell.* New York: Sun Dial Press, 1945.

———. *The Silence of History.* New York: Doubleday, 1963.

———. *Sound of a City.* New York: Paperback Library, 1962.

———. *Studs Lonigan.* New York: Signet, 1965.

———. *This Man and This Woman.* New York: Vanguard, 1951.

———. *What Time Collects.* New York: Dell, 1965.

———. *When Boyhood Dreams Come True.* New York: Signet, 1953.

———. *When Time Was Born. New York: The Smith, 1966.*

———. *A World I Never Made.* New York: Popular Library, 1960.

———. *Yet Other Waters.* New York: Vanguard, 1952.

Fast, Howard. *The Naked God.* New York: Praeger, 1957.

Freeman, Joseph. *An American Testament.* New York: Farrar and Rinehart, 1936.

Fried, Lewis. "The Naturalism of James T. Farrell." Diss. University of Massachusetts, 1969.

Frohock, William. *The Novel of Violence in America.* Dallas: Southern Methodist University Press, 1957.

Frank, Pierre. "The Fourth International." *Intercontinental Press,* 10 (serialized from #10 throught #22, 1972).

Gardiner, Harold, ed. *Fifty Years of the American Novel.* New York: Scribner's, 1952.

Gelfant, Blanche. *The American City Novel.* Norman: University of Oklahoma Press, 1954.

Gilbert, James. *Designing the Industrial State.* Chicago: Quadrangle, 1972.

———. *Writers and Partisans.* New York: John Wiley and Sons, 1968.

Glicksberg, Charles I. "The Criticism of James T. Farrell." *Southwest Review,* 35 (Summer, 1950), pp. 189-196.

Gold, Mike. *The Hollow Men.* New York: International, 1941.

———. *A Literary Anthology.* New York: International, 1972.

———. *The Mike Gold Reader.* New York: International, 1954.

Grattan, C. Hartley. "James T. Farrell: Moralist." *Harper's,* 209 (October 1954), 93-98.

Gurko, Leo. *The Angry Decade.* New York: Harper, 1947.

Harrison, John R. *The Reactionaries.* New York: Schocken, 1968.

Hart, Henry, ed. *American Writers' Congress.* New York: International, 1935.

———, ed. *The Writer in a Changing World.* New York: Equinox Press, 1937.

Halper, Albert. *Good-bye, Union Square.* Chicago: Quandrangle, 1970.

Hicks, Granville. *I Like America.* New York: Modern Age, 1938.

———. *John Reed.* New York: Macmillan, 1936.

———. *The Great Tradition.* New York: Macmillan, 1935.

———. *Part of the Truth.* New York: Harcourt, 1965.

———. *Where We Came Out.* New York: Viking, 1955.

———, et al., eds. *Proletarian Literature in the United States.* New York: International, 1935.

Hook, Sidney. *From Hegel to Marx.* Ann Arbor: University of Michigan, 1962.

———, ed. *John Dewey: Philospher of Science and Freedom.* New York: The Dial Press, 1950.

———. "The *Modern Quarterly,* A Chapter in American Radical History." *Labor History,* 10 (Spring 1974), 241-249.

———. "Some Memories of John Dewey." *Commentary,* 14 (September 1952), 245-253.

———. *Towards the Understanding of Karl Marx.* New York: John Day, 1933.

Howe, Irving, and Coser, Lewis. *The American Communist Party.* New York: Praeger, 1962.

Howe, Irving. *The Decline of the New.* New York: Horizon, 1970.

————. "Literary Criticism and Literary Radicals." *American Scholar,* 4 (Winter 1971-72), 113-120.

————. *Steady Work.* New York: Harvest, 1966.

Jacobs, Paul. *Is Curley Jewish?* New York: Atheneum, 1965.

Josephson, Matthew. *Infidel in the Temple.* New York: Knopf, 1967.

Kadushin, Charles. *The American Intellectual Elite.* Boston: Little, Brown and Company, 1974.

Kazin, Alfred. *On Native Grounds.* New York: Reynal and Hitchock, 1942.

————. *Starting Out in the Thirties.* New York: Atlantic, 1965.

Kempton, Murray. *Part of Our Time.* New York: Delta, 1955.

Lamont, Corliss, ed. *Dialogue on John Dewey.* New York: Horizon Press, 1959.

Lasch, Christopher. *The Agony of the American Left.* New York: Vintage, 1968.

————. *The New Radicalism in America.* New York: Vintage, 1967.

Lenin, V. I. *On Literature and Art.* Moscow: Progress, 1967.

Levy, Norman. "The Radicalization of Dwight Macdonald." Master's Thesis, University of Wisconsin, 1966.

Lynch, William J. "The Theory and Practice of the Literary Criticism of James T. Farrell." Diss. University of Pennsylvania, 1966.

Lyons, Eugene. *The Red Decade.* New York: Bobbs-Merrill, 1941.

McCarthy, Mary. *Cast a Cold Eeye and The Oasis.* New York: Signet, 1963.

————. *The Company She Keeps.* New York: Dell, 1964.

————. *On the Contrary.* New York: Noonday, 1967.

Macdonald, Dwight. *Memoirs of a Revolutionist.* New York: Meridian, 1963.

Madden, David, ed. *Talks with Authors.* Carbondale: Southern Illinois University Press, 1968.

————. *Proletarian Writers of the Thirties.* Carbondale: Southern Illinois University Press, 1968.

Mangione, Jerre. *The Dream and the Deal.* Boston: Little, Brown and Company, 1972.

Marx, Karl, and Engels, Frederick. *On Literature and Art.* New York: International, 1947.

Mitchell, Richard. "James T. Farrell's Scientific Novel." Diss. Syracuse University, 1963.

Morrow, Felix. *Revolution and Counter-Revolution in Spain.* New York: Pathfinder Press, 1974.

Muste, A.J. *The Essays of A. J. Muste.* Indianapolis: Bobbs-Merrill, 1967.

Neagoe, Peter, ed. *Americans Abroad.* The Hague, Holland: Servire Press, 1932.

Novack, George, ed. *America's Revolutionary Heritage.* New York: Pathfinder Press, 1976.

Novack, George. *Pragmatism Versus Marxism: An Appraisal of John Dewey's Philosophy.* New York: Pathfinder Press, 1975.

———. "Traditions and Guiding Ideas of the Socialist Workers Party in Defense Activities." *Defense Policies and Principles of the Socialist Workers Party.* New York: Socialist Worker's Party, 1968.

North, Joseph, ed. *New Masses: An Anthology of the Rebel Thirties.* New York: International, 1969.

Owen, David H. "A Pattern of Pseudo-Naturalism: Lynd, Mead and Farrell." Diss. State University of Iowa, 1950.

Panichas, George, ed. *The Politics of Twentieth-Century Novelists.* New York: Apollo, 1974.

Peck, David. "The *New Masses.*" Diss. Temple University, 1968.

Pells, Richard. *Radical Visions and American Dreams.* New York: Harper and Row, 1973.

Podhoretz, Norman. *Making It.* New York: Bantam, 1969.

Rahv, Philip. *Literature and the Sixth Sense.* Boston: Houghton Miflin, 1970.

Robbins, Jack. *The Birth of American Trotskyism.* Privately published, 1973.

Reiter, Irene Morris. "A Study of James T. Farrell's Short Stories and Their Relation to His Longer Fiction." Diss. University of Pennsylvania, 1964.

Roskolenko, Harry. *When I Was Last on Cherry Street.* New York: Stein and Day, 1965.

Rideout, Walter. *The Radical Novel in the U.S.* New York: Hill and Wang, 1966.

Salzman, Jack, and Wallenstein, Barry, eds. *Years of Protest.* New York: Pegasus, 1967.

Sanders, David. "Pattern of Rejection: Three American Novelists and the Communist Literary Line, 1919-1949." Diss. U.C.L.A., 1956.

Schneider, Isador. *The Judas Time.* New York: Dial, 1946.

Shachtman, Max. *Behind the Moscow Trial.* New York: Pioneer, 1936.

———. "Twenty-five Years of American Trotskyism." *New International,* 20 (#1, 1954), 11-25.

Shannon, David, *The Decline of American Communism.* New York: Harcourt, 1959.

———. *The Socialist Party of America.* Chicago: Quadrangle, 1967.

Simon, Rita, ed. *As We Saw the Thirties.* Urbana: University of Illinois Press, 1967.

Starobin, Joseph. *American Communism in Crisis.* Boston: Harvard University Press, 1972.

Sussman, Warren I. "The Thirties." *The Development of an American Culture.* Ed. Stanley Coben and Lorman Ratner. Englewood Cliffs, N.J.: Prentice-Hall, Inc., 1970, pp. 179-218.

Swados, Harvey. *The American Writer and the Great Depression.* New York: Bobbs-Merrill, 1966.

———. *Standing Fast.* New York: Ballentine, 1970.

Trachtenberg, Alan, ed. *Memoirs of Waldo Frank.* Boston: University of Massachusetts Press, 1973.

Trotsky, Leon. *The Case of Leon Trotsky.* New York: Merit, 1968.'

———. *In Defense of Marxism.* New York: Pathfinder, 1973.

———. *Literature and Revolution.* Ann Arbor: University of Michigan Press, 1967.

———. *My Life.* New York: Merit, 1970.

———. *On Literature and Art.* New York: Merit, 1971.

———. *The Third International After Lenin.* New York: Pioneer, 1957.

Venkataramani, M. S. "Leon Trotsky's Adventure in American Radical Politics, 1935-37." *International Review of Social History,* 9 (Part 1, 1964), 2-46.

Walcutt, Charles C. *American Literary Naturalism, A Divided Stream.* Minneapolis: University of Minnesota Press, 1956.

Wald, Alan M. "Edmund Wilson's Encounter With Marxism." *International Socialist Review,* 35 (September 1974), 32-39.

————. "Herbert Solow: Portrait of a New York Intellectual." *Prospects: An Annual Journal of American Cultural Studies,* 3 (December 1977), 418-460.

————. "Farrell and Trotskyism." *Twentieth Century Literature,* 22 (February 1976), 90-104.

————. "James T. Farrell at 70." *Praxis: A Journal of Radicalism and the Arts,* 1 (Spring 1975), 142-146.

————. "Memories of the John Dewey Commission: Forty Years Later." *Antioch Review,* 35 (Fall 1977), 438-451.

————. "The *Menorah* Group Moves Left." *Jewish Social Studies,* 38 (Summer-Fall 1976), 289-320.

————. "Mike Gold and the Radical Literary Movement of the 1930s." *International Socialist Review,* 34 (March 1973), 34-37.

————. "The Pilgrimage of Sherry Mangan: From Aesthete to Revolutionary Socialist." *Pembroke Magazine,* 8 (1977), 85-98.

————. "Revolutionary Intellectuals: *Partisan Review* In the 1930s." *Occident,* 8 (Spring 1974), 118-133.

Warren, Frank. *Liberals and Communism.* Bloomington: Indiana University Press, 1966.

Weber, Sara. "Recollections of Leon Trotsky." *Modern Occasions,* 2 (Spring 1972), 181-194.

Westlake, Neda M. "The James T. Farrell Collection at the University of Pennsylvania." *American Book Collector,* 11 (Summer 1961), 21-23.

Wolfe, Bernard. *Memoirs of a Not Altogether Shy Pornographer.* New York: Doubleday, 1972.

Wyndham, Francis, and King, David. *Trotsky: A Documentary.* Middlesex, England: Penguin, 1972.

Index